FLOOD 2010

Chronicled by The Tennessean

THE TENNESSEAN
TENNESSEAN.COM

Published by Pediment Publishing, a division of The Pediment Group, Inc. www.pediment.com Printed in Canada

TABLE OF CONTENTS

Foreword...4

The rain comes 7

Rivers Crest 29

Landmarks..59

The Community Responds...83

The Aftermath..127

FOREWORD

Everyday heroes lift our city

The rain falls.
And we rise.
The flood comes.
And we rise.
The water recedes.
And we rise.

Even in the face of the Flood of 2010, why would we expect any less of ourselves and our city? Lifelong residents and newcomers alike understand: Nashville has a heart and a soul. We are at our best when things are at their worst. And we take care of our own.

We took Mother Nature's best shot and survived. A once-in-a-lifetime flood may have knocked us down, but we got back up. And we are better for it.

This is a classic Nashville success story. You bring a guitar to town in hopes that one day you'll make it in country music. You pull a group of investors together and try to build a health-care empire. We dream big and we live large.

OK, this wasn't easy. By Sunday, May 2, we hardly recognized our city because of unprecedented rainfall. The Cumberland River was climbing out of its banks. Riverfront Park was in the river. Creeks that ran through quiet neighborhoods became swollen and dangerous. Entire residential communities were underwater.

Even with the latest technology in weather forecasting, nobody saw this coming. The two-day total of more than 13 inches of rain nearly doubled the previous 48-hour record of 6.68 inches in the wake of Hurricane Frederic in 1979.

Dark, murky water covered parts of downtown. Thousands were without power. Some residents had to leave their homes as the water rose. Others couldn't because of flooded streets and washed-out bridges.

The three interstates that run through Nashville were closed at times. Motorists were stranded for about 15 hours at a rest area on westbound Interstate 40 at mile marker 172 near the Dickson exit.

Middle Tennesseans are notorious for hurrying to the nearest supermarket and draining it of essentials at the first whisper of snow or ice. But what do you do when the parking lot of the local grocery is under 2 feet of water and the power is out?

City's routine changed

New words and terms became part of our vocabulary — flood plain, river elevation, dam releases, emergency response.

The flood didn't play favorites. A city filled with special destinations and familiar sights took on water. And it hurt to watch.

Nashville is a diverse city, but there is a shared sense of ownership. You may not know the difference between Bach and bluegrass, but it's hard not to be proud of the gleaming Schermerhorn Symphony Center. The Country Music Hall of Fame and Museum is a vital part of our city, even to those who aren't country music fans. Both suffered significant flood damage.

And it didn't stop there. Anything remotely near the Cumberland River was at risk. That included the Gaylord Opryland Resort & Convention Center, where guests were evacuated last Sunday. Many of them spent the night sleeping on cots at McGavock High School.

Gaylord CEO and Chairman Colin Reed said it could be six months before the hotel can reopen. It was another reminder that our routine had changed.

Some people visit the sprawling hotel every December to look at the Christmas lights. Some bring out-of-towners there to walk through the atriums and enjoy the sights. Some make it a regular stop for Sunday brunch.

Barbara Buchanan considers Opryland Hotel part of her life. A native Nashvillian, she now lives in suburban Chicago with her husband and two children. Her high school prom was at Opryland Hotel. Her wedding was at Opryland Hotel. Her family comes back every other year to vacation at Opryland Hotel.

She was scheduled to stay at the hotel for three days in mid-June. Those vacation plans have been scuttled.

"When I heard about the flood, my first thought was, 'Opryland is near that river. I hope it's OK,' " she said. "Then I saw the pictures and it just broke my heart. It's such a beautiful place."

Everyone was in search-and-rescue mode. Dozens of residents of River Plantation subdivision in Bellevue were forced from their homes and had to spend the night at nearby Nashville Christian Academy. They showered in the athletic locker room facility.

"The community was incredible," said Ben Martin, athletics director at Nashville Christian.

Fishermen and water enthusiasts used their boats to conduct impromptu rescues. Brian Sullins of Antioch called it the Redneck Armada. He and several of his fishing buddies worked the flooded Mill Creek area to get stranded homeowners out of harm's way.

"We're just a bunch of guys that know how to get a boat from here to there," said Sullins, who estimated that he ferried 40 people to safety Sunday and Monday.

'This is a special city'

In time, the floodwaters subsided, but the sense of community didn't. Out of shared tragedy came a shared commitment to help one another. Within three days of the flood, more than 12,000 people signed up to help Hands On Nashville, the agency coordinating volunteer disaster relief. And that didn't include the volunteer efforts by neighborhoods, schools, churches and individuals.

"Neighbors are checking on neighbors, seeing if there's anything they can do to help," Mayor Karl Dean said. "This is a special city. We're lucky to live here."

Fundraising efforts kicked in quickly. Country music star and longtime Nashville resident Vince Gill hastily put together a telethon on WSMV-TV. Among the stars who performed was Keith Urban, who played a borrowed guitar because his equipment was destroyed in the flood. More than $1.7 million was raised in 3½ hours.

At first, the national media didn't get it. Compared with the oil spill in the Gulf of Mexico and a failed car bombing in Times Square, a flooded city wasn't deemed sexy enough.

Finally, on Monday night, Keith Olbermann gave a shout-out to Nashville and the surrounding area on MSNBC's Countdown. Other news outlets eventually came along for the ride. Anderson Cooper of CNN hit town Thursday and repeatedly apologized for his late arrival. By then, the Cumberland River had long since crested and the worst damage was over.

Want bigger national headlines? Start looting.

The absence of major looting was a significant part of this story. We're better than that. Our city never lost control.

A natural disaster brought out our very best. Volunteer spirit was on display throughout the Volunteer State. Neighbors helped neighbors. Good Samaritans were everywhere. If you needed help, all you had to do was ask.

There were heroes at every turn, Regular Joes and Janes who reached out to help those in need. Everybody seemed willing to pitch in, whether it was stacking sandbags to reinforce the levee at MetroCenter, clearing debris as the floodwaters receded or simply making sure your neighbors were OK.

Now comes the hard part. We may have been through the worst of this but much work remains as we clean up and rebuild.

But we'll manage. Because this is Nashville.

David Climer / The Tennessean

THE RAIN COMES

The rain just wouldn't stop. For two days, Tennessee saw roads turn to rivers. Water inundated homes, cars and businesses — leaving some with only their roofs showing like islands. Boats became rescue vehicles. Thousands were forced to evacuate; others were trapped watching as water crept up their porches. Leaving home became a salvage operation.

The flood of 2010 broke records, shut down highways, cut off power, forced flight cancellations and left billions of dollars of damage. Gov. Phil Bredesen asked for federal disaster relief. Drenched police officers guided people who had no sense or no choice but to be on the roads. Firefighters and emergency workers answered calls nonstop and saved lives. People saw TV sets, shoes, toys and memories drift out their doors. Some lost heart.

Thousands of cars, homes and basements were filled with water. With entire neighborhoods submerged, hundreds of people were in shelters. But neighbors checked on neighbors, churches and colleges opened doors to those with nowhere to go, and people shared advice and misery while waiting for the sun to return. The effects of this devastation would last for days, weeks and months to come.

"This situation is going to require a very large recovery process," Dean said. "The magnitude of the damage to our community was much more than what I expected. ... The safety of some of our infrastructure is questionable."

By Sunday night the Cumberland River was expected to crest at 50 feet. Forty feet is the official flood level. Officials said that at 51 feet, the floodwaters would reach the LP Field parking lot and possibly the stadium. At 55 feet, areas of Lower Broadway and First Avenue would be endangered.

In Williamson County, Franklin Mayor John Schroer issued a state of emergency and a curfew for residents. Parts of the city were flooded Saturday, then the waters receded, only to come back Sunday with more intense rains.

Theresa Phillips, who waded out of her Gallatin neighborhood through chest-high water, tried to put the flood into perspective.

"I've been out there 15 years, and this is the worst. I'm sure we lost everything we have, but we got out alive."

Meg Downey / The Tennessean

MAY 1, 2010 (left) A trucker passes by a flooded car as flood waters cover I-24 near the Antioch Pike overpass. One person died Saturday when vehicles were caught in floodwaters on Interstate 24 near Bell Road, *LARRY MCCORMACK*

MAY, 2010 (right top) Captain Barry Micghael with the Jackson Police department walks out across South Highland Ave. on the first day of flooding. *MARIANN MARTIN/JACKSON SUN*

MAY 1, 2010 (right bottom) Ray Bartlett, a resident at Nashville I-24 Campground in Smyrna, helps clean up after flooding at the campground. *JOHN A. GILLIS/DAILY NEWS JOURNAL*

MAY 1, 2010 (below) Flooding at the corner of Rocky Fork Road and Tedder Boulevard in Smyrna. *JOHN A. GILLIS/DAILY NEWS JOURNAL*

MAY 1, 2010 (bottom) Old Nashville Highway closed near Sam Ridley Parkway due to flooding. *JOHN A. GILLIS/DAILY NEWS JOURNAL*

MAY 1, 2010 (above) Marven Ortiz and Jose Perez take a break to check on the rising waters of Mill Creek that had already flooded the basement in their Wimpole Dr. home. *LARRY MCCORMACK*

MAY 1, 2010 (above) Brent Reed,13, tries to save flowers from the flooding at his grandparent's store, Reed's Produce Market & Garden Center in downtown Franklin. *SHELLEY MAYS*

MAY 1, 2010 (left top) Andrea Silva, a Beech High School graduate, and Jamey Howell, a soon-to-be Beech High School graduate, clung to Howell's Jeep as flood waters overtook the vehicle at the intersection of Saundersville Road and Lower Station Camp Creek. *RICK MURRAY*

MAY 1, 2010 (left bottom) Tracy Reed of Reed's Produce Market & Garden Center walks through water inside his store to remove produce and the cash registers from the downtown Franklin business. *SHELLEY MAYS*

MAY 1, 2010 (opposite left top) Flood waters bring out the curious to take photos and see a site that no one has seen since the flood of 1979, the Dairy King on Thompson Lane underwater. 'I've never seen it come up this fast' said owner Jeff Jones. He and 'an army of friends' got most of the equipment out as the flood waters rose. *LARRY MCCORMACK*

MAY 1, 2010 (opposite left bottom) City of Franklin new police department lower level parking garage, flooded. *SHELLEY MAYS*

MAY 1, 2010 (opposite right) Police allowed truckers, one at a time, to pass through flood waters on I-24 near Antioch Pike. One person died when vehicles were caught in floodwaters on Interstate 24 near Bell Road. *LARRY MCCORMACK*

MAY 2, 2010 (above) Cars, boats and tractor trailers litter the pavement on I-24 Eastbound toward Murfreesboro. The interstate was closed in both directions. *TOM STANFORD*

MAY 2, 2010 (right) Cars and trucks litter the highway on I-24 eastbound Sunday morning. The wooden structure to the left is the porch of the building that floated down I-24 according to TDOT workers on the scene. *TOM STANFORD*

MAY 2, 2010 (far right) A driver takes on high water at Burgess Lane and Port Royal Road in Spring Hill Sunday, May 2, 2010. *SANFORD MYERS*

MAY 2, 2010 (top) Friends and family members work together to clear the area in Selmer on Sunday May 2, 2010, the day after an EF-2 tornado hit the area. *MARIANN MARTIN/JACKSON SUN*

MAY 2, 2010 (above) Fallen tree at Cason Lane and Windemere Drive. *JOHN A. GILLIS/DAILY NEWS JOURNAL*

MAY 2, 2010 (left) Friends and family members stand in the rubble of a moblie home in Pocahontas, TN on Sunday May 2, 2010 where Liz Buxton was killed after a storm hit the area. *MARIANN MARTIN/JACKSON SUN*

MAY 2, 2010 (above) Flooding at West Main Street and Bridge Avenue. *JOHN GILLIS/DAILY NEWS JOURNAL*

MAY 2, 2010 (opposite left top) Joe Presley is cleaning his father-in-law's grave as Bethesda Presbyterian Church barely stands in Purdy. The building in the back is Bethesda Presbyterian Church which was hit by a tornado at the beginning of May of 2010. The church was completely torn down on May 15. *MARIANN MARTIN/THE JACKSON SUN*

MAY 2, 2010 (opposite left middle) A resident looks at the storm water runoff as he surges past at Burgess Lane and Port Royal Road in Spring Hill. *SANFORD MYERS*

MAY 2, 2010 (opposite left bottom) These cars were submerged on Waddell Hollow Road in Liepers Fork. *SANFORD MYERS*

MAY 2, 2010 (opposite right) A man walks down W. Central Street in Trenton, TN after heavy rains caused streets to flood in the city and throughout Gibson County.

MAY 2, 2010 (opposite top) Home owner Tim Rodgers builds up his homemade dam around his air conditioning units as storm runoff moves through his yard at his home in Spring Hill. His neighbor wasn't as lucky as flood waters went into his crawl space and garage. *SANFORD MYERS*

MAY 2, 2010 (opposite bottom left) Greg Lebel tries to divert water into a flood drain so it wouldn't flood his yard on Riverside Dr in East Nashville. *JOHN PARTIPILO*

MAY 2, 2010 (opposite bottom right) Ricky Cook, left, tries to save equipment from his West Nashville back yard with some help from Brandon McCain. *SHELLEY MAYS*

MAY 2, 2010 (above) A rock slide left Highway 96 west impassible in both directions in Franklin. *SANFORD MYERS*

MAY 2, 2010 (right top) Terrell Perkins watches the water rush through his front yard on Geneva Street in East Nashville. *JOHN PARTIPILO*

MAY 2, 2010 (right bottom) Chris Green stands in the driveway of his grandmother's home in East Nashville. *JOHN PARTIPILO*

MAY 2, 2010 (above) Dover Anthony sings as he overlooks the parking lot of submerged cars at the Knights Motel in East Nashville. *JOHN PARTIPILO*

MAY 2, 2010 (left) An NES crew pumps water from below a street drain on River Front. *JOHN PARTIPILO*

MAY 2, 2010 (far left) Ira Godsy who lives in the Knights Motel in East Nashville wades out to his car. Most of the cars were underwater. *JOHN PARTIPILO*

MAY 2, 2010 (top) The water line from Saturday's flood on the Lebanon town sqaure is evident as attorney Robert MacPherson prepares to nail the door shut. *LARRY MCCORMACK*

MAY 2, 2010 (above) Sandbags couldn't stop the water from coming in businesses on Lebanon's square on Saturday. *LARRY MCCORMACK*

MAY 2, 2010 (left) Water covers the warning signs put up to close the road on Caldwell Lane in Hendersonville. More flooding is expected as flood waters rise all around the midstate. *LARRY MCCORMACK*

MAY 2, 2010 (above) Roy Turner holds a blanket closely around him as he waits in a shelter at the Gallatin Civic Center. He and other family members had to wade out of their Blade Road home as the waters rose in Gallatin. Turner said the water was chest deep as he waded out. 'And I'm 6 foot 2.' More flooding is expected as flood waters rise all around the midstate. *LARRY MCCORMACK*

MAY 2, 2010 (right) Millie White 75, waits in a shelter at Richland Community Church for family members to pick her up after her West Nashville home was damaged by the flood . *SHELLEY MAYS*

MAY 2, 2010 (far right) Donald Sweat and Sarah Tippett take photos of a railroad bridge that was washed off its foundations in Lebanon.
LARRY MCCORMACK

MAY 2, 2010 (below) Jeff Garbin and Gene Graham light candles at a shelter at Richland Community Church. The West Nashville Church had no power.
SHELLEY MAYS

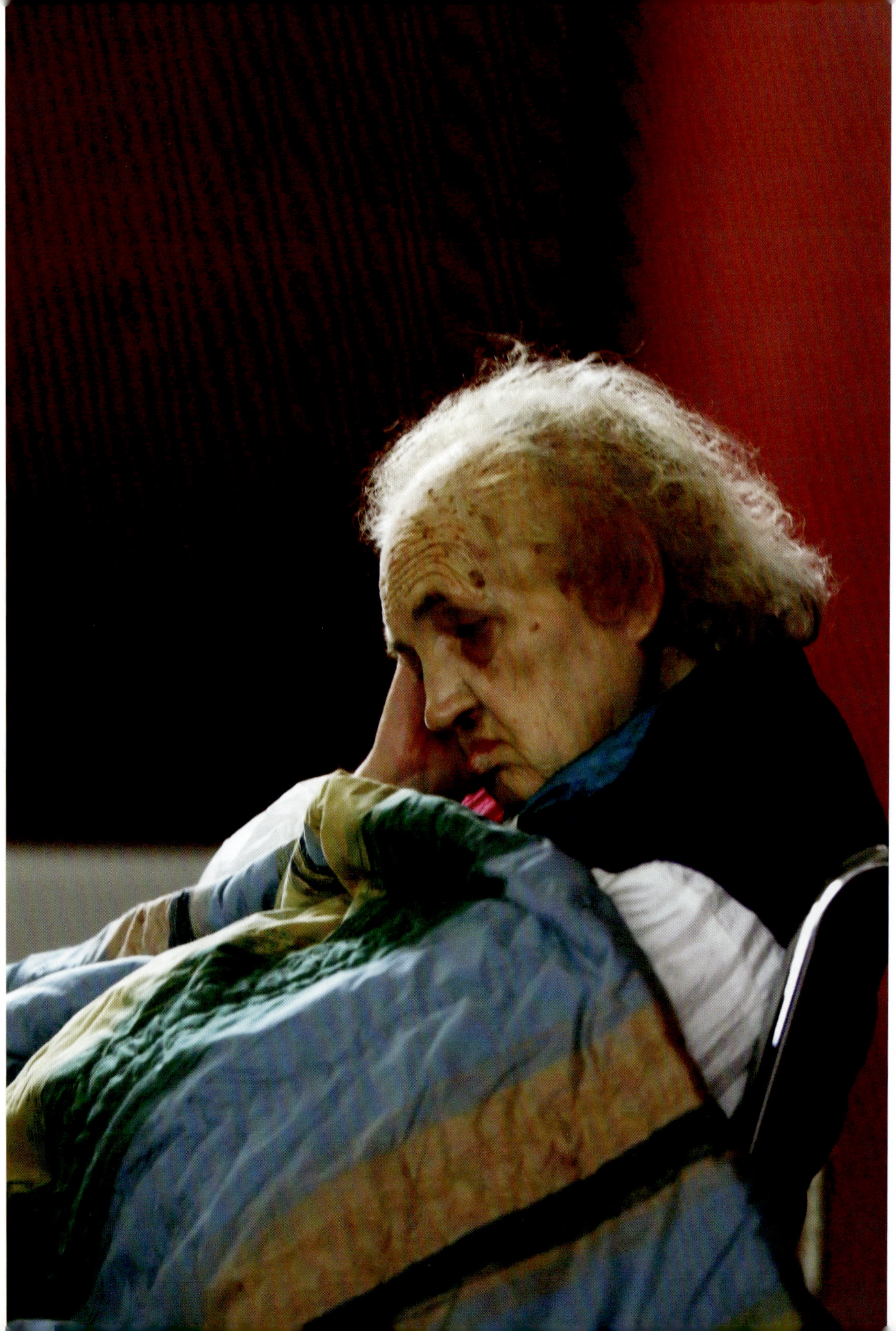

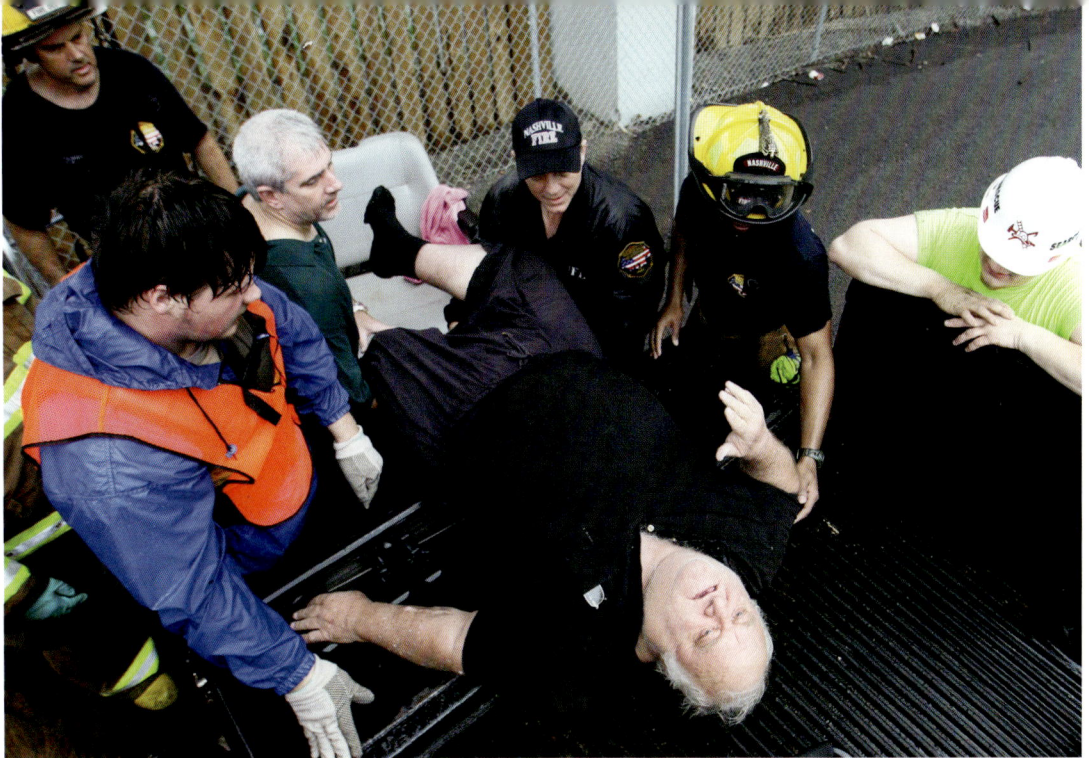

MAY 2, 2010 (previous left) Metro Fire Department Special Operation rescues a Belle Meade police officer off Harding Road in Belle Meade. Police officer Norm Shelton was clinging to a tree for an hour before being rescued. The location of his patrol car is unknown. *SHELLEY MAYS*

MAY 2, 2010 (previous right top) Ron Dunavant is helped by volunteers and Metro firemen into a flat bed truck after his home was flooded. Dunavant waited for two hours for ambulance on Winn Road in West Nashville home on Sunday May 2, 2010. *SHELLEY MAYS*

MAY 2, 2010 (previous right bottom) Neighbors carry Janie Cramen to an ambulance after she was rescued by boat from her West Nashville home on Sunday May 2, 2010. Cramen is on oxygen. *SHELLEY MAYS*

MAY 2, 2010 (right) Macey Broadway, 4, along with her family, survey the damage on Steammill Ferry Road, off Riverside Dr., in Bemis, TN after severe weather hit the area. *BETH SPAIN/THE JACKSON SUN*

MAY 2, 2010 (far right) Ryan Clark, a TSU student, looks at the car that is almost underwater near his home on Blakemore Ave. *SHELLEY MAYS*

RIVERS CREST

On a day when the Cumberland River continued to rise, crippling Middle Tennessee neighborhoods, businesses and several of Nashville's iconic music, sports and tourist spots, the most critical threat Monday night was that floodwaters would knock out the city's drinking supply.

The river crested downtown at close to 52 feet, four feet higher than expected. That was the highest it had been since 1937.

As sandbag crews worked furiously into the evening, the city's remaining water treatment plant was perilously close to being flooded. Such a turn would have cast the historic flood of 2010 into a new level of crisis for more than 600,000 residents across Davidson County, and Brentwood, which relies on Metro's water.

With the waters still on the rise, officials were still largely in rescue mode across the region.

"Anybody who gets in a helicopter, you can see it's enormous," said Gov. Phil Bredesn, who formally requested federal emergency assistance while touring the 52-county disaster area. "It's a lot of damage. This is not $5 million. This is going to be a very, very expensive thing."

Another potentially devastating problem hanging over the city was a leaking levee at MetroCenter, north of downtown. State and Metro workers placed sandbags along the levee. The residents and businesses in the area were evacuated. Among the businesses threatened was Second Harvest food bank, which had millions of dollars worth of food stored in a warehouse.

From the air, the pervasiveness of the flood came into focus. Whole streets and neighborhoods were underwater. Shopping centers, like Opry Mills, were submerged, and industrial businesses along the river had equipment tossed and twisted around by the river's current. There were stretches where all that could be seen was a lonely farmhouse roof poking from the waters.

According to the National Weather Service, Nashville crested Monday evening, but for cities downriver on the Cumberland, such as Ashland City, Clarksville and Dover, the crest was expected Tuesday and Wednesday. In Clarksville, the waters on Monday were already 15 feet above flood levels.

The Army Corps of Engineers, which manages the dam system that is designed to control the flow of waters along the Cumberland and its tributaries, said the storm was the most intense since the dam system was completed more than three decades ago.

Brad Schrade and Nate Rau / The Tennessean

MAY 1, 2010 (left) A high water sign rests on a pole at the Cumberland RiverWalk May 3, 2010. *GREG WILLIAMSON/THE LEAF-CHRONICLE*

MAY 2, 2010 (above) The Salvation Army on Kraft Street in Clarksville.
GREG WILLIAMSON/THE LEAF-CHRONICLE

MAY 1, 2010 (opposite top left) Katie Stephens carries out merchandise as her father Joe Stephens goes back in to his Riverside Drive American Flower Gift shop to retrieve more items. *GREG WILLIAMSON/THE LEAF-CHRONICLE*

MAY 2, 2010 (opposite bottom left) The Red River spilled over College Street flooding Clarksville Towing, The Jukebox and several other businesses and cut off St. Bethlehem residents from downtown Clarksville. *GREG WILLIAMSON/THE LEAF-CHRONICLE*

MAY 2, 2010 (left) The Cumberland River flood at the corner of Riverside Drive and Providence Boulevard, covered the Two Rivers Center in Clarksville.
GREG WILLIAMSON/THE LEAF-CHRONICLE .

MAY 2, 2010 (below) Businesses at the corner of Riverside Drive, North Second Street and Kraft Street under water. *GREG WILLIAMSON/THE LEAF-CHRONICLE*

MAY 2, 2010 (right top) Looking south on Riverside Dr. Multiple businesses were affected in The Riverview Center. *GREG WILLIAMSON/THE LEAF-CHRONICLE*

MAY 3, 2010 (opposite) Rhonda Hand gives David Francescon a hug after he gave her a ride on his boat so she could check on her home and pets in the Somerset Farms development off of Coley Davis Road in Bellevue. *SANFORD MYERS*

MAY 3, 2010 (right bottom) Samantha Smith, 15, sits in the garage of her home that was badly damaged by flood waters in the Somerset Farms subdivision of Coley Davis in Bellevue Monday. *SANFORD MYERS*

MAY 3, 2010 (middle bottom) Lou Hanemann pulls his family, wife, Natalie, holding Mae, 20 months, and his son Merritt, 6, from their flooded home in the Somerset Farms development off of Coley Davis in Bellevue. *SANFORD MYERS*

MAY 3, 2010 (below) Jenny Tygard walks through deep water with some of her belongings after flood waters devastated the Poplar Ridge condos off of Coley Davis Road in Bellevue. *SANFORD MYERS*

MAY 3, 2010 (right top) A fire truck drives past parked cars and trucks on 70S at Coley Davis Road as the sun burns through a morning fog in Bellevue Monday. *SANFORD MYERS*

MAY 3, 2010 (opposite top) David Francescon pilots his boat as he takes Rhonda Hand back to her home in the Somerset Farms development off of Coley Davis Road in Bellevue. Hand is a nurse and hadn't been home to check on it in over 24 hours. *SANFORD MYERS*

MAY 3, 2010 (opposite right) Tourist Robert Evan looks out onto First Ave. in downtown as flood waters continue to rise on Monday morning. *JOHN PARTIPILO*

MAY 3, 2010 (opposite bottom) Alfredo Varela walks through high water after trying to get into his friends new home in the River Bridge development off of Coley Davis Road in Bellevue. His friends were out of town getting furniture for their new home. The home was badly flooded as well as the car. Varela returned later with a key and rescued a wedding gown. The owners are getting married in June. *SANFORD MYERS*

MAY 3, 2010 (below) The Nashville Skyline from the sky. *SAMUEL M. SIMPKINS*

MAY 3, 2010 (above) Residents use a newly built bridge to get over to the Interstate 40 side from Coley Davis Road. The bridge was built by residents Lee Scott, Matt Nicholson and TVA worker Jason Burch with donated materials from Home Depot. *SANFORD MYERS*

MAY 3, 2010 (left) Residents off of Coley Davis Road deal with the aftermath of the retreating flood waters in Bellevue. *SANFORD MYERS*

MAY 3, 2010 (opposite) Fast moving flood waters destroyed these train tracks behind the Poplar Ridge Condos off of Coley Davis Road in Bellevue. *SANFORD MYERS*

MAY 3, 2010 (above) Cars and several town homes were badly damaged at the River Bridge development off of Coley Davis Road in Bellevue. *SANFORD MYERS*

MAY 3, 2010 (right top) Volunteers sandbag at Metrocenter as the Cumberland River rises in Nashville, TN. *DIPTI VAIDYA*

MAY 3, 2010 (bottom right) Cathy Carrick talks to the insurance company after she and some helpers had ripped the soaked carpet out of her flooded home in the River Bridge development off of Coley Davis Road in Bellevue. Carrick was not covered for the flood. *SANFORD MYERS*

MAY 3, 2010 (opposite top left) Daniel Selfridge stands in his living room that the flooding demolished. 'This is all we've got,' said a resident, who said they desperately needed some assistance to get them on their feet again. All trailers were uprooted and destroyed, one trailer drifted down a creek. *DIPTI VAIDYA*

MAY 3, 2010 (opposite top right) Daniel Selfridge prepares to camp out with other men to guard what remains of their possessions at the Trailer Rest Trailer Park on Nolensville Road near the fairgrounds in Nashville, TN. *DIPTI VAIDYA*

MAY 3, 2010 (opposite bottom right) T. W. Hale helps his friends vacuum water out of the Pilcher Building in downtown as flood waters continue to rise. *JOHN PARTIPILO*

MAY 3, 2010 (opposite bottom left) Vu Nguyen cleans mud from inside his house after flood waters were over a foot high inside at the Somerset Farms development off of Coley Davis Road in Bellevue. *SANFORD MYERS*

MAY 3, 2010 (right top) Volunteers sandbag at Metrocenter as the Cumberland River rises Monday evening in Nashville, TN. *DIPTI VAIDYA*

MAY 3, 2010 (right bottom) Chip McDonald, right, gets some help from friend Daniel Moore as they lift his refrigerator back up after flood waters had knocked it over in his home in Somerset Farms off of Coley Davis Road in Bellevue. *SANFORD MYERS*

MAY 3, 2010 (below) A view of First Ave. looking at the river in downtown as flood waters continue to rise. *JOHN PARTIPILO*

MAY 3, 2010 (above) Phil Martin watches as Randall Bains vacuums out water from the Pilcher Building in downtown as flood waters continue to rise. *JOHN PARTIPILO*

MAY 3, 2010 (above) Beth Hammock takes a picture out the window overlooking First Ave. and the river in downtown as flood waters continue to rise. *JOHN PARTIPILO*

MAY 3, 2010 (right) Spectators look at downtown Nashville. This photo taken from the Shelby Street Pedestrian Bridge over the Cumberland River. *LARRY MCCORMACK*

MAY 3, 2010 (opposite right) A kayaker paddles under the Shelby Street Bridge as flood waters rise around the riverfront area of downtown Nashville. *LARRY MCCORMACK*

MAY 3, 2010 (oppisite top) The rising floodwaters fill downtown as flood waters continue to rise. *JOHN PARTIPILO*

MAY 3, 2010 (opposite bottom) Trail West employee A.J. Jefferson swims to the lower area of the store. He was trying to get in to move stock from the ground floor to higher floors. *LARRY MCCORMACK*

MAY 3, 2010 (left) Spectators look at downtown Nashville from the Shelby Street Pedestrian Bridge over the Cumberland River. *LARRY MCCORMACK*

MAY 3, 2010 (far left) The flood waters rise around the riverfront area of downtown Nashville. *LARRY MCCORMACK*

MAY 3, 2010 (below) Three people walk through the water that has submerged Second Ave. as the flood waters rise around the riverfront area of downtown Nashville. *LARRY MCCORMACK*

MAY 3, 2010 (above) Spectators look at downtown Nashville from the Shelby Street Pedestrian Bridge over the Cumberland River. *LARRY MCCORMACK*

MAY 3, 2010 (left) Lower part of downtown Nashville is filled as water continues to rise from the Cumberland River. *LARRY MCCORMACK*

MAY 3, 2010 (right top) A view from above looking out over First Ave. in downtown as flood waters continue to rise. *JOHN PARTIPILO*

MAY 3, 2010 (right middle) Industrial businesses that back up to the Cumberland River from the sky. The water is reported to be still rising. *SAMUEL M. SIMPKINS*

MAY 3, 2010 (right bottom) A boat rests in a tree near Blue Hole Road. *SHELLEY MAYS*

MAY 3, 2010 (opposite) Geary Falk wades behind girlfriend Kathy Gray's house in the Greenland Farms subdivision Monday as they attempt to pump flood water from the basement. *BETH LIGGETT/THE LEAF-CHRONICLE*

MAY 3, 2010 (right) Flood waters rise around the riverfront area of downtown Nashville. *LARRY MCCORMACK*

MAY 3, 2010 (opposite) A man walks through a flooded Second Ave as the flood waters rise around the riverfront area of downtown Nashville. *LARRY MCCORMACK*

MAY 3, 2010 (below) Spectators look at downtown Nashville. Photo taken from the Shelby Street Pedestrian Bridge over the Cumberland River. *LARRY MCCORMACK*

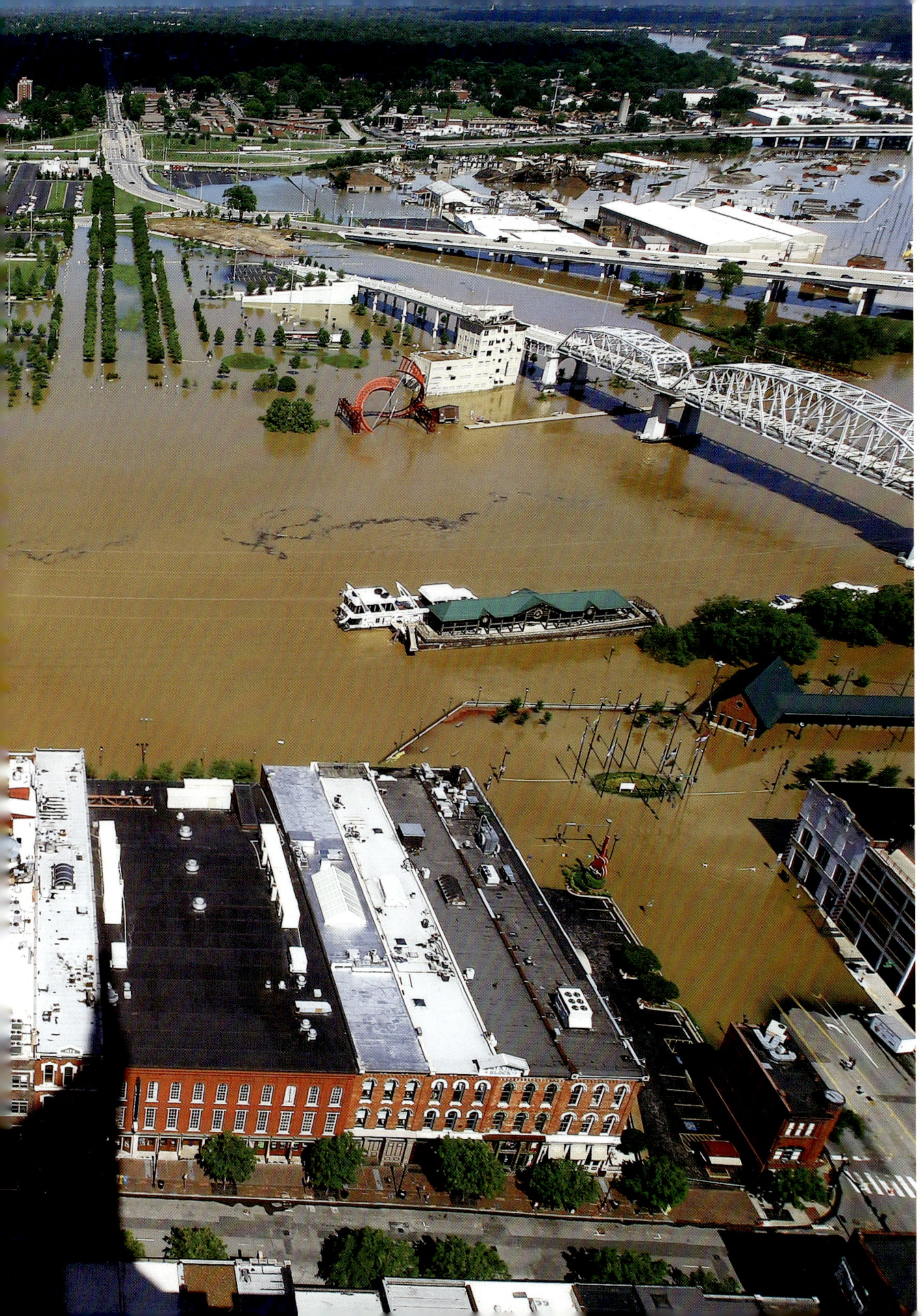

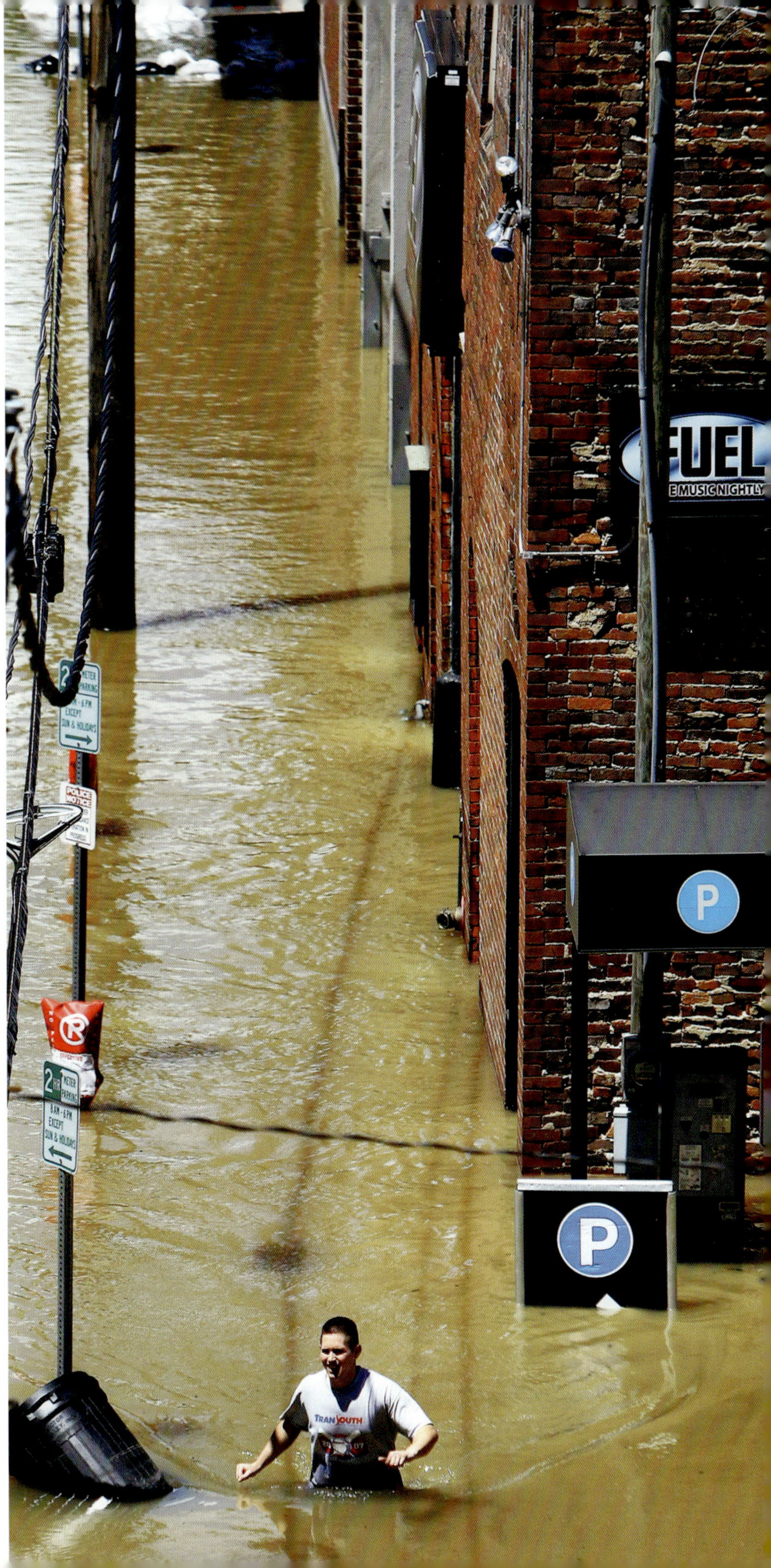
FUEL
P
P

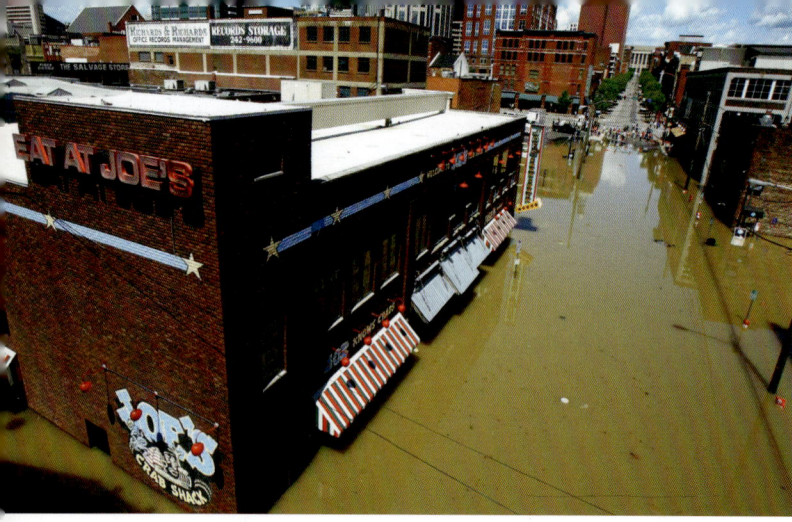

MAY 3, 2010 (above) Water surrounds Joe's Crab Shack in downtown Nashville as water from the Cumberland River makes its way into the city center. *LARRY MCCORMACK*

MAY 3, 2010 (right top) Spectators look at downtown Nashville from the Shelby Street Pedestrian Bridge over the Cumberland River. *LARRY MCCORMACK*

MAY 3, 2010 (right bottom) Lighthouse Christian School senior Dillon Chambliss removed a damaged soccer goal from the school's athletic fields which were submerged during the flood. Baseball uniforms hang on a fence to dry out. One of the school's buildings made the national news after it was filmed floating down a Nashville interstate. *SHELLEY MAYS*

MAY 3, 2010 (opposite) Phil Martin walks on First Ave. in downtown as flood waters continue to rise. *JOHN PARTIPILO*

MAY 4, 2010 (above) Hodges Brothers Cars got most of their cars out before the flood waters filled the lot. The high waters of the Cumberland River crested at 62.58 feet above flood stage and began to slowly recede throughout the day. *ROBERT SMITH/THE LEAF-CHRONICLE*

MAY 4, 2010 (left) Metro police officers were called to the Clarksville Pike bridge after an officer on Youngs Lane thought he saw a person on top of debris floating down the Cumberland River in Nashville. After some tense moments it was determined that it was this queen size bed with pillows floating down the river. *SANFORD MYERS*

MAY 4, 2010 (far left) As the flood waters recede, there are trucks resting under water on Pumping Station Rd. *SAMUEL M. SIMPKINS*

MAY 4, 2010 (above) Spectators gather as the U.S. Army Corps of Engineers release water from Percy Priest Dam. *LARRY MCCORMACK*

MAY 4, 2010 (above) Gaylord Springs® Golf Links from the sky. *SAMUEL M. SIMPKINS*

MAY 4, 2010 (left) A crane walks near one of the greens at the Tom Rhodes golf course. *JOHN PARTIPILO*

MAY 4, 2010 (far left) Mercer Adams tries his luck as the U.S. Army Corps of Engineers was releasing water from Percy Priest Dam. 'The current's just too strong' he said. *LARRY MCCORMACK*

MAY 4, 2010 (right) Houses on Southern Parkway that back up against Highways 48 & 13 received flood damage from the rising backwaters. The high waters of the Cumberland River, which crested at 62.58 feet above flood stage, began to slowly recede throughout the day. *ROBERT SMITH/THE LEAF-CHRONICLE*

MAY 4, 2010 (below) Woodstock subdivision in Clarksville looked more like a lake than a residential neighborhood. *GREG WILLIAMSON/THE LEAF-CHRONICLE*

MAY 7, 2010 (bottom) Olga M. Beddingfield talks on the roof overlooking the dam at Old Hickory Dam in Hendersonville, TN. *SAMUEL M. SIMPKINS*

MAY 5, 2010 (opposite) A worker attaches a hose as he and others pump flood water away from buildings between First and Second in downtown Nashville. *LARRY MCCORMACK*

LANDMARKS

The historic flood of 2010 struck Nashville's tourism industry at its heart, taking out a signature hotel and other attractions just as the city entered its peak summer visitor season.

• The flooded Gaylord Opryland Resort & Convention Center would not reopen for several months, leaving Nashville without 12 percent of its hotel rooms and wiping out as much as a fourth of the convention business that comes to town.

• Honky-tonks and shops along Lower Broadway and on Second Avenue, including the Wildhorse Saloon and Hard Rock Cafe, closed Monday and didn't know when they would reopen because of flooding in their basements.

• At one point, LP Field resembled a swimming pool as flood waters filled the field. Bridgestone Arena had to pump water out of its main level, where flood levels reached about a foot. The arena benefited from the fact that no events are planned at the arena until later in the month.

• By Monday afternoon, water had risen to the third row of the subterranean Ford Theater at the Country Music Hall of Fame and Museum. The Grand Ole Opry has rescheduled shows to the Ryman Auditorium and War Memorial Auditorium, former homes to the Opry. The last time the Opry had to relocate was in 1975, when it temporarily moved to Municipal Auditorium, also because of Cumberland River flooding.

• The Schermerhorn Symphony Center was closed indefinitely as damage was more extensive than originally reported. Although the concert floor was spared, the basement has all the mechanical equipment of the building and a $2.5 million pipe organ and two pianos were severely damaged.

Most would bounce back in time for the CMA Music Festival on June 10-13, if not well before then, said Butch Spyridon, president and CEO of the Nashville Convention & Visitors Bureau.

But Gaylord Opryland, with its nearly 2,900 hotel rooms and 600,000 square feet of meeting and exhibition space, would be out of commission indefinitely.

The resort on the banks of the Cumberland River evacuated 2,000 guests and employees Sunday night as the rain-filled river rose, flooding the Delta and Cascades atriums. By Monday, the Cascades seafood restaurant and lobby were underwater.

Bonna Johnson / The Tennessean

MAY 3, 2010 (left) The Schermerhorn Symphony Center is surrounded by water in downtown Nashville as water continues to rise from the Cumberland River. *LARRY MCCORMACK*

MAY 2, 2010 (above) Opryland employees gather up sheets, blankets and pillows after evacuated guests left McGavock High school. *JOHN PARTIPILO*

MAY 2, 2010 (right) Hundreds of hotel guests are evacuated out of the Opryland Hotel after hotel officials were concerned about the flooding in the area. *JOHN PARTIPILO*

MAY 2, 2010 (far right) The Delta portico was completely under 10-19 feet of water. Many of the plants are rare and will have to be replaced. *JOHN PARTIPILO*

MAY 2, 2010 (right top) At one of the loading docks at the Opryland Hotel diesel fuel was in the river water from flood waters going over the electrical generators. *JOHN PARTIPILO*

MAY 2, 2010 (right bottom) Danny Covington, the head of maintenance at the Schermerhorn Symphony Center, checks the water level in one of the hallways. The basement is completely filled with water and has extensive damage. *JOHN PARTIPILO*

MAY 2, 2010 (opposite) At The Waters Edge restaurant is under the water at the Delta Portico at Opryland. *JOHN PARTIPILO*

MAY 2, 2010 (left bottom) All of this flood water leaked into the Schermerhorn Symphony Center. The basement is full of water. *JOHN PARTIPILO*

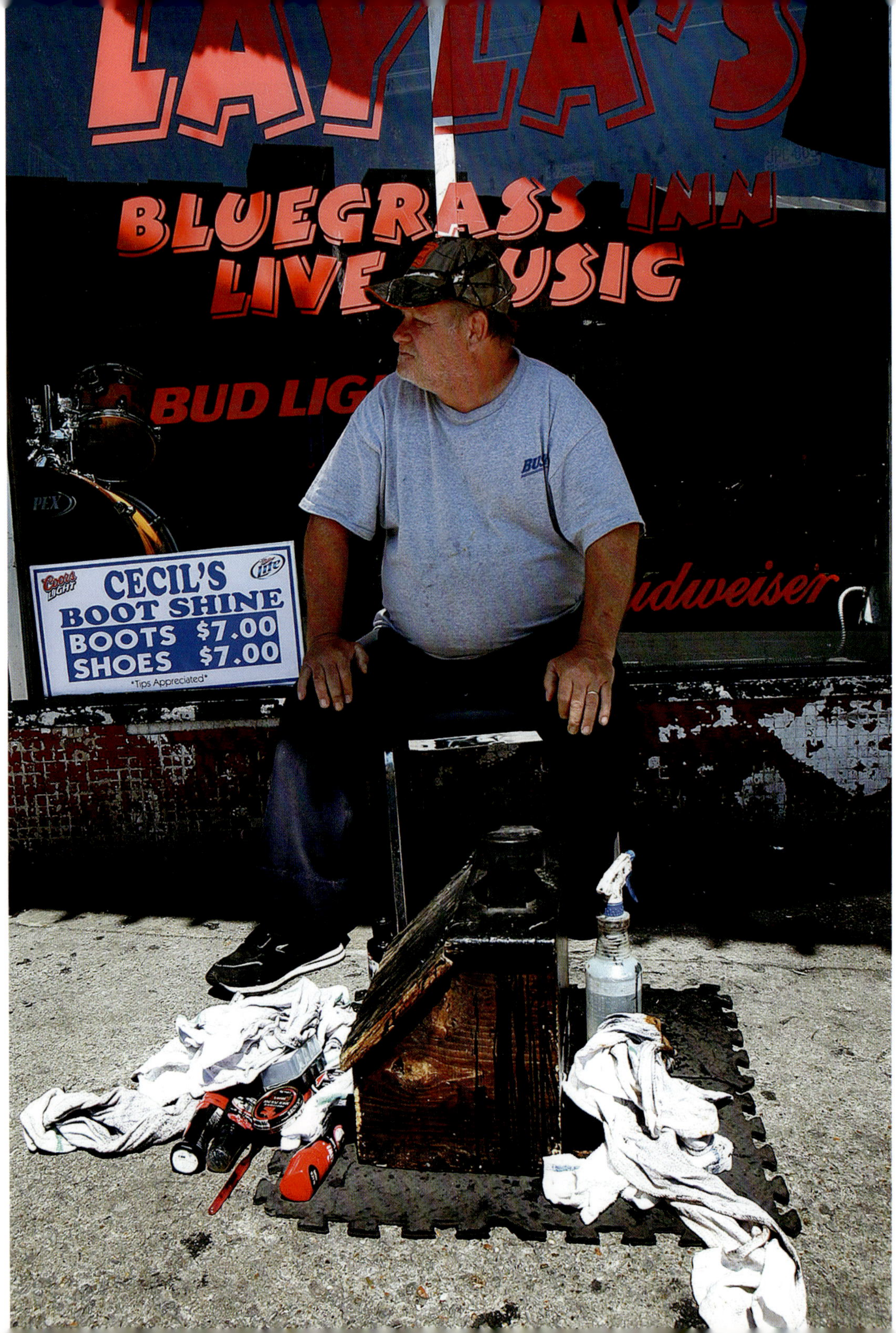
LAYLA'S
BLUEGRASS INN
CECIL'S
BOOT SHINE
BOOTS $7.00
SHOES $7.00
Tips Appreciated

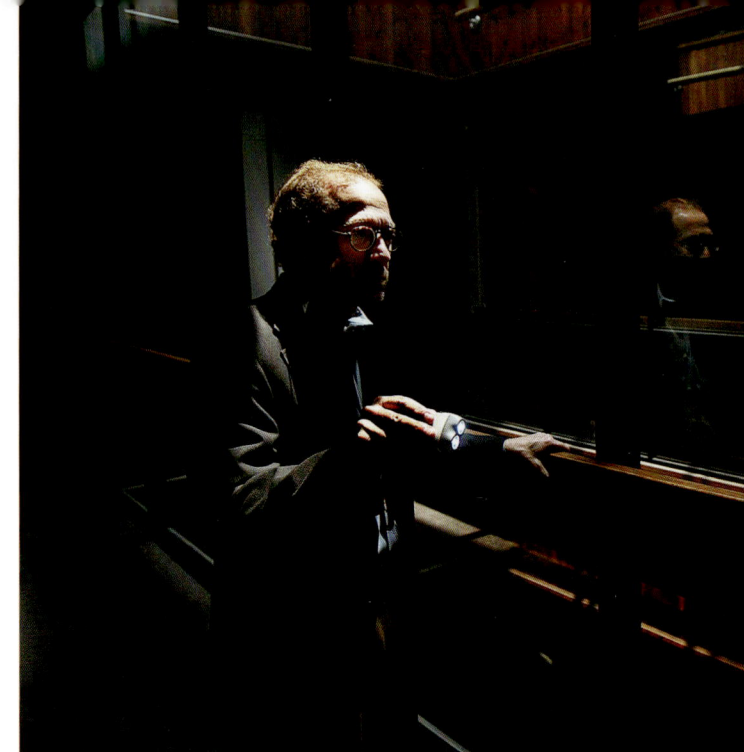

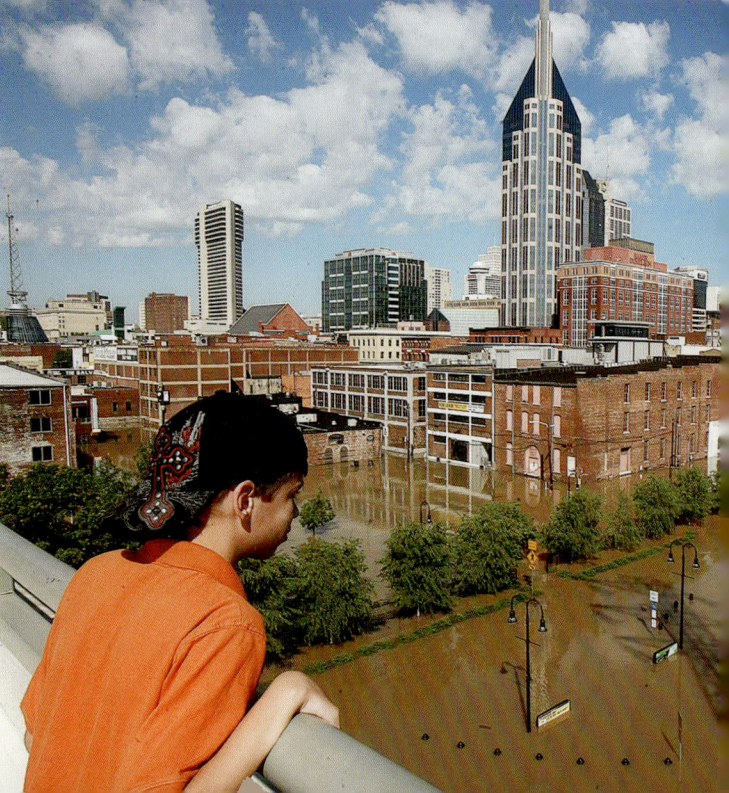

MAY 3, 2010 (above) A woman walks past the Schermerhorn Symphony Center in downtown Nashville. *LARRY MCCORMACK*

MAY 2, 2010 (left top) Attorney David O. Huff uses a flashlight down the hallway to his office at the Pilcher Building on 2nd Ave. The building lost power and the elevator was full of water. *JOHN PARTIPILO*

MAY 2, 2010 (left bottom) Trent Burian, 12, looks over downtown Nashville from the Pedestrian bridge. *JOHN PARTIPILO*

MAY 2, 2010 (right) Corey Carlough of the Lee Company said he has pumped over 70,000 gallons of water out of the Country Music Hall of Fame. *JOHN PARTIPILO*

MAY 2, 2010 (opposite) Street shoe shine man Cecil Duke said he only shined one pair of shoes all day on lower Broadway. *JOHN PARTIPILO*

MAY 3, 2010 (left) Workers move sandbags around the Country Music Hall of Fame as the flood waters rise around the riverfront area of downtown Nashville. *LARRY MCCORMACK*

MAY 3, 2010 (right) The Country Music Hall of Fame is surrounded by water in downtown Nashville as water continues to rise from the Cumberland River. *LARRY MCCORMACK*

MAY 3, 2010 (below) Liz Thiels of the Country Music Hall of Fame surveys the flooding inside the Ford Theater at the Country Music Hall of Fame. *LARRY MCCORMACK*

Due to flooding in the downtown area, The Country Music Hall of Fame and Museum will be closed today. We apologize for the inconvenience.

MAY 3, 2010 (opposite) Waters rise around the Country Music Hall of Fame and other buildings around the riverfront area of downtown Nashville. *LARRY MCCORMACK*

MAY 3, 2010 (above) Workers and contractors survey the rising flood waters that now cover the floor of the Bridgestone Arena in downtown Nashville. *LARRY MCCORMACK*

MAY 4, 2010 (right) Pennington Bend, near Gaylord Opryland from the sky. *SAMUEL M. SIMPKINS*

MAY 3, 2010 (far right) Flood waters surround LP Field as the flood waters rise around the riverfront area of downtown Nashville. *LARRY MCCORMACK*

MAY 3, 2010 (below) Opry Mills Mall with Gaylord Opryland in the background from the sky. *SAMUEL M. SIMPKINS*

MAY 11, 2010 (above) Disaster clean-up crews are removing water from the Schermerhorn Symphony Center which was damaged by the downtown flooding. *SHELLEY MAYS*

MAY 6, 2010 (opposite left) Gerry Senechal, Associate Director of Music, sweeps the dirt from the sanctuary floor as dehumidifiers take out the moisture from St. George's Episcopal Church. Water ran through parts of the church and up to 18 inches in the kindergarten. Workers began to move furniture and materials to higher ground. Belle Meade Police Department set up a command center on the second floor of the church since city hall, next door to the church, was also flooded, said Belle Meade City Manager Beth Reardon. *LARRY MCCORMACK*

MAY 7, 2010 (opposite right top) Gaylord Entertainment President David Kloeppel (left) and CEO Colin Reed held a press conference to give an update after the flood at Opryland Hotel in Nashville, TN. *MANDY LUNN*

MAY 11, 2010 (opposite right bottom) Opry Mills Mall in the process of cleaning up from the flood in Nashville, TN. *DIPTI VAIDYA*

73

MAY 13, 2010 (above) The keys of the stage piano are mud-stained during flood clean-up at the Grand Ole Opry in Nashville, TN. *DIPTI VAIDYA*

MAY 11, 2010 (left) Debris pile near the Grand Ole Opry. *SHELLEY MAYS*

MAY 11, 2010 (far left) Outside Gaylord Orpyland Hotel furniture, appliances, mattresses, and doors have been removed and placed in a pile after flood waters damaged the first floor of the hotel. The resort sits adjacent to the Cumberland River and is protected by levees built to sustain 100-year-flood standard. *SHELLEY MAYS*

MAY 12, 2010 (opposite) The Grand Ole Opry entrance after floodwaters receded. *SHELLEY MAYS*

MAY 13, 2010 (above) Pete Fisher, Vice President and General Manager of the Grand Ole Opry, talks with Jon Mire, Technical Services Manager during flood clean-up at the Grand Ole Opry in Nashville, TN. *DIPTI VAIDYA*

MAY 13, 2010 (opposite) Workers clean around a statue of Bill Monroe in the lobby after the flood at the Grand Ole Opry in Nashville, TN. *DIPTI VAIDYA*

MAY 12, 2010 (left) Maher Abdelnor and his family share the porch with neighbor boy Yousseb Samy. Abdelnor lost everything in the flood and to make matters worse he worked at the Opryland Hotel and is also out of work until the hotel goes back to normal. *JOHN PARTIPILO*

MAY 13, 2010 (bottom left) A damaged dressing room during flood clean-up at the Grand Ole Opry in Nashville, TN. *DIPTI VAIDYA*

MAY 13, 2010 (bottom right) The stage has been stripped down during flood clean-up at the Grand Ole Opry in Nashville, TN. *DIPTI VAIDYA*

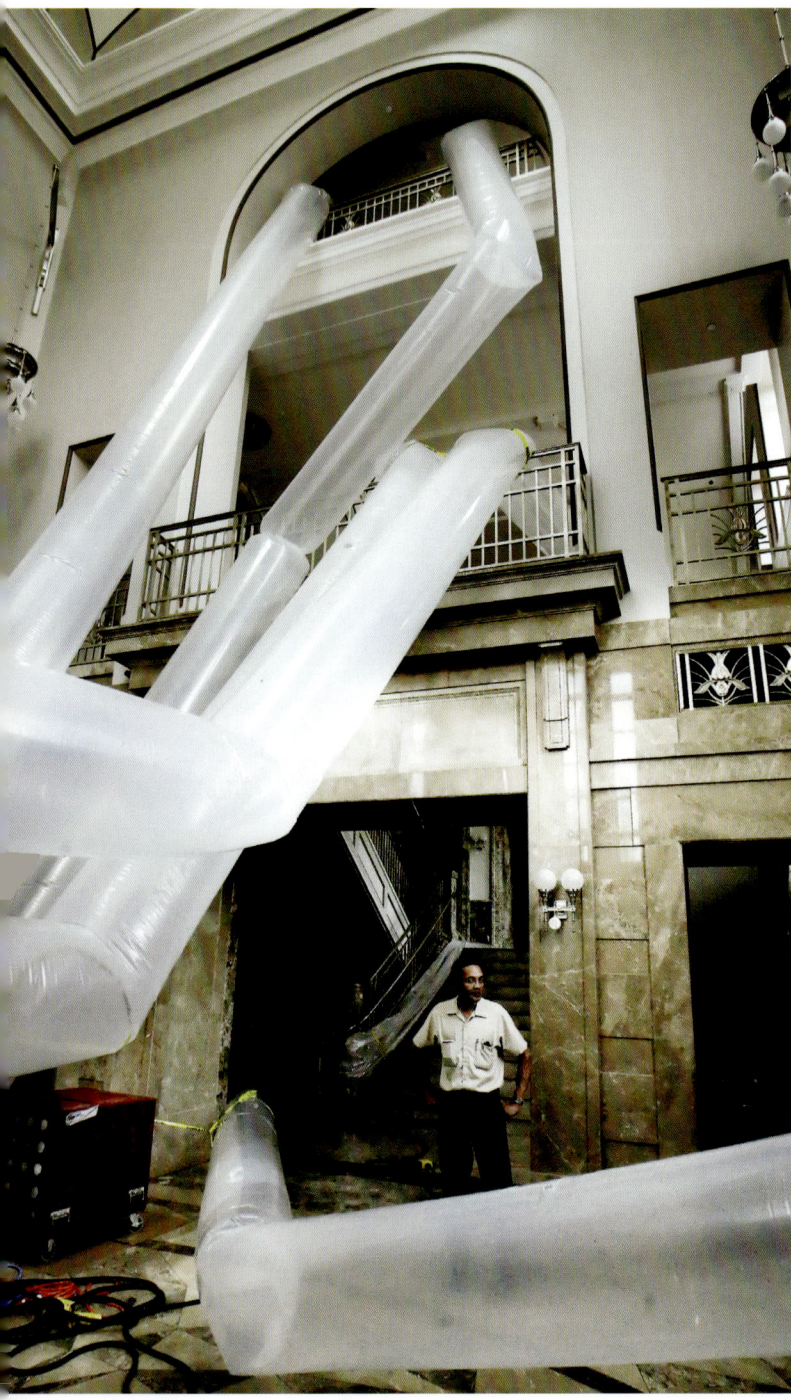

MAY 13, 2010 (top) Workers are cleaning furniture, dishes, and even hangers outside the Schermerhorn Symphony Center. *SHELLEY MAYS*

MAY 13, 2010 (above) Rows of chairs sit in the Schermerhorn Symphony Center's basement which was underwater due to flooding. *SHELLEY MAYS*

MAY 13, 2010 (left) Schermerhorn Symphony Center facility maintenance technician Ray Creech stands among restoration air tubing in one of the Schermerhorn Symphony Center's lobbies after the basement was damaged by the extensive flooding. *SHELLEY MAYS*

MAY 13, 2010 (right) Air tubes snake around one of Schermerhorn Symphony Center's lobbies. *SHELLEY MAYS*

MAY 13, 2010 (left) Mike Walker of Regancy DKI gives a tour of Schermerhorn Symphony Center's basement which was damaged by the extensive downtown flooding. Although the concert floor was spared, the basement has all the mechanical equipment of the building, including the air conditioning system, electrical switching, storage areas and the kitchen. *SHELLEY MAYS*

MAY 13, 2010 (far left) Plastic covers the organ pipes inside the Schermerhorn Symphony Center's concert hall which was not damaged by the flooding. *SHELLEY MAYS*

MAY 13, 2010 (below) Mike Walker of Regancy DKI gives a tour of Schermerhorn Symphony Center's basement which was underwater due to flooding. *SHELLEY MAYS*

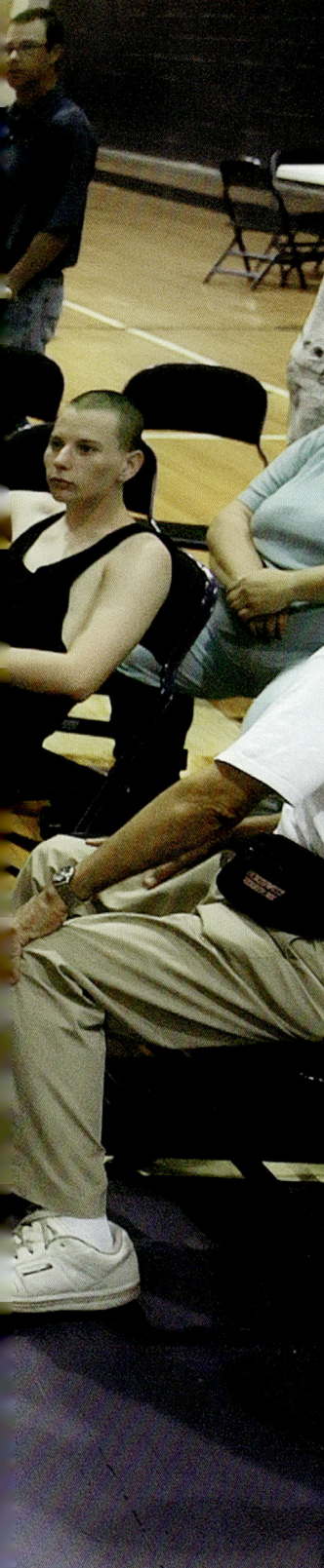

THE COMMUNITY RESPONDS

One was a dessert baker. Another was a physical trainer. A third was a pastor. They had different skills, not at all related to flood cleanup. But it didn't matter.

Pockets of the hardest-hit communities — East Nashville, Antioch, West Nashville, Bordeaux, Bellevue — came up for air to find an outpouring of workers from churches, volunteer groups and disaster relief agencies.

Volunteers fed workers, tore out drywall, counseled distraught flood victims, handed out cases of water and tweeted on Twitter about what help was needed. They made a dent in work that will go on for months.

"There was life-changing damage," said Catherine McTamaney, a volunteer organizer in East Nashville. "People are realizing how much work needed to be done. The numbers of volunteers just kept climbing through the week."

The American Red Cross had recorded more than 1,300 volunteers by Friday. Large congregations saw members show up en masse like Cross Point Community Church, which had more than 1,600 people on Saturday.

Hands On Nashville saw more than 5,100 volunteers log more than 19,000 hours to help out across the city by Saturday.

"The referrals we have made far outnumber the people we have signing up just through us," said Lisa Davis, external affairs director for Hands On Nashville. "It's really neat to see the way the whole community is organizing and coming together."

In communities like East Nashville — where many people don't think word got out that the flood affected them — neighbors were taking volunteerism in their own hands. Water had damaged homes in historic Lockeland Springs, East Nashville and Inglewood.

Linda Cato, who has lived in her Russell Street home for 33 years, was reluctant to accept help, but the overwhelming job ahead of her changed her mind.

"It makes you want to cry," said Cato, choking back tears as 14 people cleaned out her basement. "You can lose something in a flash, but then you have the most wonderful people showing up like this."

A lot more skilled labor will be needed as Nashville and surrounding counties begin to rebuild.

"Entire neighborhoods are just gone," said Brian Williams, executive director for Hands On Nashville. "To rebuild those neighborhoods is going to take months."

Christina E. Sanchez / The Tennessean

MAY 5, 2010 (left) Larry Gatlin plays for people that were displaced by the flood at the Red Cross shelter at Lipscomb University. *JOHN PARTIPILO*

MAY 3, 2010 (above) A Red Cross shelter resident and animal rescue volunteer from Kingston Springs brought 15 dogs and one cat to the Lipscomb University shelter after her home was damaged by water. At this Red Cross shelter people can bring their family cats and dogs. *SHELLEY MAYS*

MAY 3, 2010 (left top) Friends, neighbors and Street Department workers pile sandbags in front of the garage door of Rosie Quintero's home in the Greenland Farms subdivision in Clarksville. *BETH LIGGETT/THE LEAF-CHRONICLE*

MAY 3, 2010 (left bottom) Metro inmates Joseph Taylor, right, and Josh VanKirk make sandbags for flooding. Fifty Davidson County Sheriff's Office inmates bagged approximately 72 tons of sand at the Correctional Services Division warehouse, 5117 Harding Place. The more than 10,000 bags were distributed, upon request, to various places throughout the city. *SHELLEY MAYS*

MAY 3, 2010 (below) Metro inmate James Pitt throws a sandbag to help flooding efforts in Nashville, TN. *SHELLEY MAYS*

MAY 3, 2010 (above) An American flag hangs on a fence to dry as Lighthouse Christian School student Noah Jackson, 12, cleans debris from his school athletic fields after they were submerged during the flood. One of the school's buildings made the national news after it was filmed floating down a Nashville interstate. Students, teachers and parents spent the day cleaning. *SHELLEY MAYS*

MAY 5, 2010 (above) Larry Gatlin plays for people who were displaced by the flood at the Red Cross shelter at Lipscomb University. *JOHN PARTIPILO*

MAY 4, 2010 (left) Andrea Silvia and Jamey Howell talk about how they survived the flood waters in Nashville, TN. *MANDY LUNN*

MAY 4, 2010 (right) Chris Young performs at the Grand Ole Opry at War Memorial Auditorium. *SHELLEY MAYS*

MAY 4, 2010 (opposite) Marty Stuart, left, greets U.S. Senator Lamar Alexander to the stage at Grand Ole Opry show at War Memorial Auditorium. The show moved from Opryland because of the flood that damaged the interior. It's the first time the Opry has been there since the 40s and the first Opry show since the flooding began. *SHELLEY MAYS*

MAY 5, 2010 (left) Volunteer Marjorie Weaver brings sandwiches and cold drinks to residents and volunteer workers as they try to clean homes on West Hamilton Rd in North Nashville. *LARRY MCCORMACK*

MAY 5, 2010 (far left) Vera Arnold, 77, has a large family that is helping her clean her flooded home in Antioch near Blue Hole Rd. *DIPTI VAIDYA*

MAY 5, 2010 (right top) Mayor Karl Dean visits with residents as they try to clean their homes from the weekend flooding on West Hamilton Rd. in North Nashville. *LARRY MCCORMACK*

MAY 5, 2010 (right bottom) Firefighter Trey Nelms and Officer Lynette Frazier with the urban search and rescue team on Mallard Drive in Nashville, TN. *DIPTI VAIDYA*

MAY 5, 2010 (below) Volunteer Dan Gislao, right, shows East Nashville resident Letta Williams digital photos of her home which was flooded to take some of the initial shock away. Williams just moved into the neighborhood a month ago and her musical instruments were spared. *JOHN PARTIPILO*

MAY 5, 2010 (above) Volunteer Jeremy Mackens loads bottled water for a resident in Erin, TN. The free water was supplied by TEMA and the Tennessee National Guard after the Houston County water treatment plant went offline because of rising floodwaters and five water mains were knocked out of service. Residents in parts of six middle Tennessee counties were urged to boil water before drinking. *SHELLEY MAYS*

MAY 5, 2010 (above) Tammy Awali hugs her mother Patti Hollingsworth as her granddaughter Aaliyah Muller, 6, watches. Volunteers helped salvage some of the personal items out of the home which was filled with water.
JOHN PARTIPILO

MAY 5, 2010 (right top) J. M. Tillman with Labor Ready assists in the clean-up of the Waterfront Deli on First Ave. in downtown Nashville, TN. *MANDY LUNN*

MAY 5, 2010 (right) A volunteer loads a case of water into Larry Simpson's vehicle during a water give away at Baily Middle School in Nashville, TN.
MANDY LUNN

MAY 6, 2010 (right) Public Works driver Titus Moore helps pick up trash from flood victims in North Nashville. *SAMUEL M. SIMPKINS*

MAY 5, 2010 (below) Josh Dipzinski assits in the clean up of a building on First Ave. in downtown Nashville, TN. *MANDY LUNN*

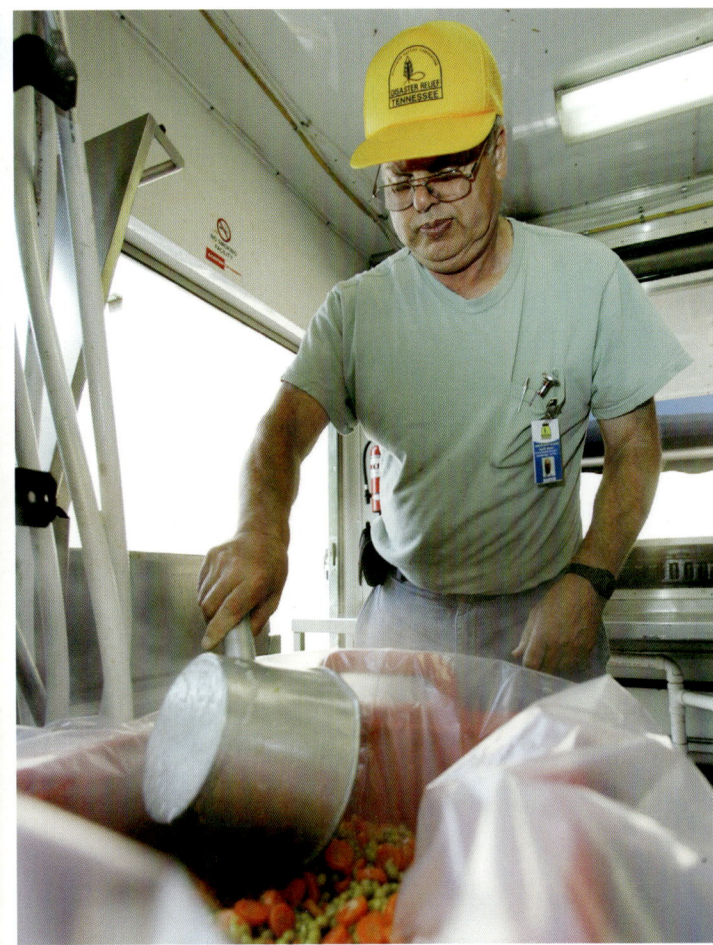

MAY 7, 2010 (above) Southern Baptist Disaster Relief volunteer Marvin Dockery prepares vegetables for flood victim meals at Judson Baptist in Nashville, TN. *MANDY LUNN*

MAY 7, 2010 (right top) As the search continues for Daniel Brown, off Elm Hill Pike along Mill Creek, father Roger Brown, from Iowa, searches the area Friday afternoon. *SAMUEL M. SIMPKINS*

MAY 7, 2010 (right bottom) Ali Hemyari, of the Davidson County Rescue Squad K-9 Unit and K-9 Roxy, Cadaver-Area Search dog, continue to search for Daniel Brown. *SAMUEL M. SIMPKINS*

MAY 6, 2010 (opposite) Some Fort Campbell soldiers tipped a shed upright in the Willowbend subdivision in Clarksville. More than 470 soldiers from Fort Campbell visited several city and county areas to help flood victims clean up. *GREG WILLIAMSON/THE LEAF-CHRONICLE*

MAY 7, 2010 (above) Steve Edwards, left, with sons William, 13, left, and Hayden, 9, right, and Mervin Troyer, all from the same church in Woodbury, scrape the water-damaged flooring in Elizabeth Zapp's home that was destroyed by the flood in Shacklett, TN. *DIPTI VAIDYA*

MAY 7, 2010 (opposite) Mac Morel, owner of Southern Sun Paving of Thompson's Station was inundated with calls to repair flood damaged driveways. He said he was getting five calls a day to come out and give estimates. Morel operates a paving machine on a driveway in Franklin. *SHELLEY MAYS*

MAY 7, 2010 (above) Clarksville Fire Rescue firefighter Gary Watson cleans the mud off the parking lot of Tony Knight's Autoplex on Riverside Drive. CFR is helping clean the debris that was left when the flood waters dropped. *ROBERT SMITH/THE LEAF-CHRONICLE*

MAY 7, 2010 (left top) Students from Harpeth Middle School and High School stand in the middle of highway 70 soliciting donations for flood victims in Shacklett, TN. *DIPTI VAIDYA*

MAY 7, 2010 (left bottom) LifePoint Hospitals volunteers Melissa Smith (left), Melody Rose and Alexandria Holloway work with Southern Baptist Disaster Relief volunteers preparing meals for flood victims at Judson Baptist in Nashville, TN. *MANDY LUNN*

MAY 7, 2010 (below) Friends and neighbors in Shacklett, TN set up their own disaster response headquarters that started with 6 loaves of bread and became a stocked tent in a church parking lot with food, water, cleaning supplies and volunteers. 'This is what we do in the country - help each other,' said one resident. *DIPTI VAIDYA*

MAY 7, 2010 (bottom) David Bers, left, gives Chris Barber and Chris Crimmings a free hug before a Nashville Symphony concert at Public Square Friday. *SHELLEY MAYS*

MAY 7, 2010 (above) Christopher Cross performing with the Nashville Symphony at Public Square for a free concert. *SHELLEY MAYS*

MAY 7, 2010 (left) Maestro Giancarlo Guerrero and the Nashville Symphony performing at Public Square for a free concert. *SHELLEY MAYS*

MAY 7, 2010 (far left) The Nashville Symphony performs a free concert at Public Square. *SHELLEY MAYS*

MAY 7, 2010 (below) Two girls dance during a free Nashville Symphony concert at Public Square. *SHELLEY MAYS*

MAY 8, 2010 (left top) Homeland Secretary Janet Napolitano speaks with Jessica Marshall and other volunteers at the Bellevue Community Center in Bellevue, TN. Along with Napolitano were Governor Phil Bredesen, Mayor Karl Dean, Senator Lamar Alexander, Congressman Jim Cooper and Senator Douglas Henry. *MANDY LUNN*

MAY 8, 2010 (left bottom) Dana Coulter scrubs pitchers and other items that were removed from Kickers, which had about five feet of flood water inside. *ROBERT SMITH/THE LEAF-CHRONICLE*

MAY 9, 2010 (above) Church members Mary and Ken Hall pray as they sit behind the flower marked pew of church members Bill and Frankie Rutledge who died in the flood waters on Harding Pike at St. George's Episcopal Church in Nashville. The Rutledges, who sat in the same pew every Sunday, were reported to be on their way to the church when the accident occurred. The church also received several inches of water during the flood. *SANFORD MYERS*

MAY 9, 2010 (right) Church members attend services at St. George's Episcopal Church which was damaged in last week's floods in Nashville. *SANFORD MYERS*

MAY 10, 2010 (right top) U.S. Department of Commerce Secretary Gary Locke talks with Mayor Karl Dean, as U.S. Housing and Urban Development (HUD) Secretary Shaun Donovan talks with Congressman Jim Cooper during a tour in downtown Nashville. The tour took a look at the damage the flood waters have done to downtown Nashville. *SAMUEL M. SIMPKINS*

MAY 10, 2010 (right bottom) Homeowner Betty Burns talks with FEMA worker Dean Brouillette before the FEMA community meeting held Monday night at Centennial High School. *LARRY MCCORMACK*

MAY 10, 2010 (bottom middle) Mayor Karl Dean speaks as U.S. Department of Commerce Secretary Gary Locke, U.S. Housing and Urban Development (HUD) Secretary Shaun Donovan and Congressman Jim Cooper listen in downtown Nashville. *SAMUEL M. SIMPKINS*

MAY 10, 2010 (below) The FEMA community meeting held Monday night at Centennial High School drew a crowd to learn about different relief options. *LARRY MCCORMACK*

MAY 10, 2010 (above) Franklin City Administrator Eric Stuckey talks to the crowd at the FEMA community meeting held Monday night at Centennial High School. *LARRY MCCORMACK*

MAY 11, 2010 (right) Landfill trash had to be sorted because of contamination by flood waters. At the Williamson County landfill, sizes increased from 300 cubic yards to about 1,000 cubic yards a day. *SAMUEL M. SIMPKINS*

MAY 11, 2010 (below) Because of the abnormal amounts and different types of trash from the storms, Robert Harrison has to untangle storm debris from a truck at the Williamson County Landfill. *SAMUEL M. SIMPKINS*

MAY 11, 2010 (left) Reverand Michael Broadnax, center, introduces speakers for the night that included Rabbi Philip Rice, left, of Congregation Micah and Imam Mohamed Ahmed, right, of the Islamic Center of Nashville as local clergy gathered at Greater Bethel AME Church on South Street for an Interfaith Unity Service to pray for Nashville's recovery. *LARRY MCCORMACK*

MAY 11, 2010 (below) SBA's Michael Lapton, left, and SBA administrator Karen Mills talk with small business owner Roger Sauve after Mills held a press conference on SBA loan programs to aid homeowners and business owners. She also opened an SBA business recovery center at Tennessee State University's downtown Avon Williams campus. *LARRY MCCORMACK*

MAY 11, 2010 (bottom) Rabbi Philip Rice of Congregation Micah chats with Imam Mohamed Ahmed of the Islamic Center of Nashville as local clergy gathered at Greater Bethel AME Church on South Street during an Interfaith Unity Service to pray for Nashville's recovery. *LARRY MCCORMACK*

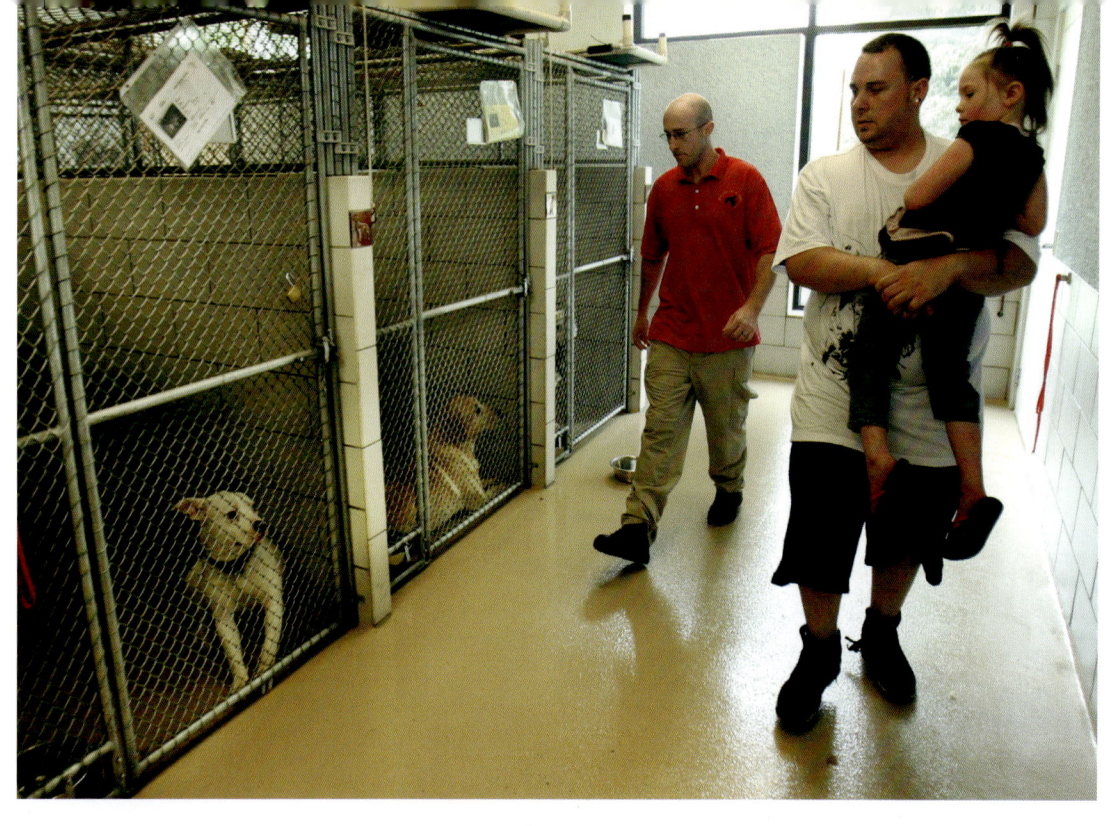

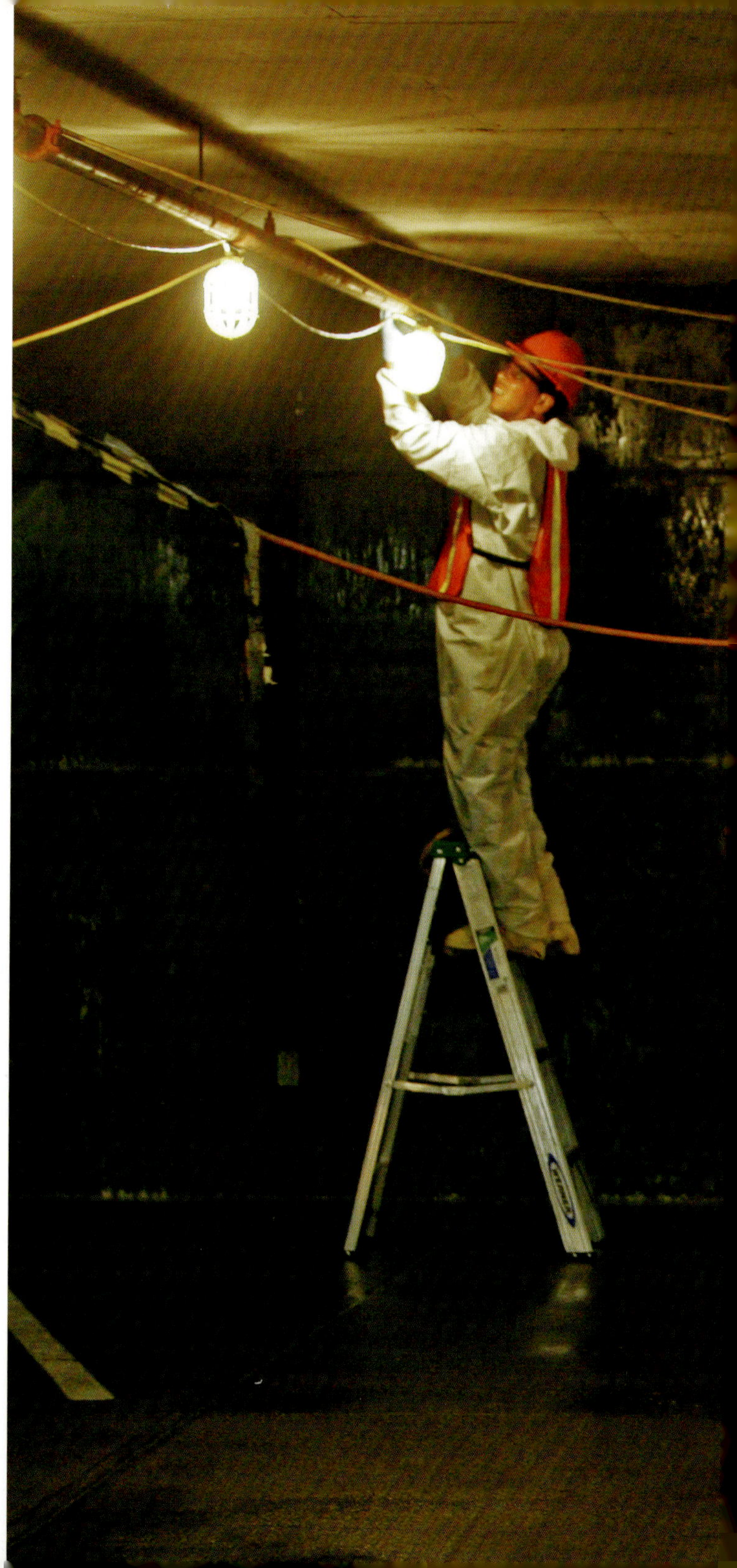

TIDY CATS
Special Kitty
Cat Litter

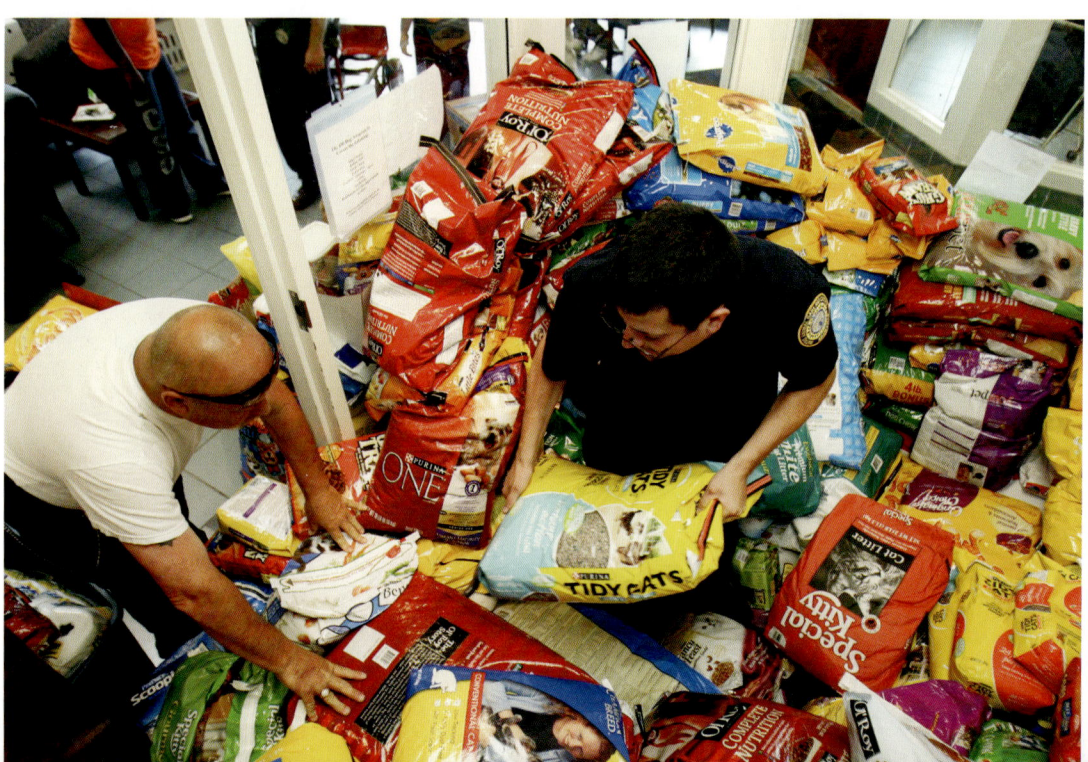

MAY 13, 2010 (left) ServPro workers continue to clean the Pinnacle Building underground parking garage after flood waters filled the garage in Nashville. *SANFORD MYERS*

MAY 12, 2010 (opposite left top) Metro Animal Care & Control Center worker Brandon Sprinkles, center, helps Wesley Smith and his daughter Brianna, 4, look for their lost dog, Tiny, in the animal shelter. Smith said all his kennels in his backyard were underwater. *SHELLEY MAYS*

MAY 12, 2010 (opposite left bottom) Metro Animal Care and Control Center's Billy Biggs, left, and Bruce Gilmore load donated cat and dog food to be delivered to flood victims in Nashville. *SHELLEY MAYS*

MAY 13, 2010 (left) ServPro workers continue to clean the Pinnacle Building underground parking garage after flood waters filled the garage in Nashville. *SANFORD MYERS*

MAY 13, 2010 (above) Gregory Dennis talks with councilman Frank Harrison about the flood. Harrison was out visiting neighborhoods and talking to people who were hit hard in the flood. *JOHN PARTIPILO*

MAY 16, 2010 (above) Dierks Bentley is projected on screen from the call center of the telethon, Music City Keep On Playin', a benefit for flood relief at the Ryman Auditorium in Nashville. *JAE S. LEE*

MAY 16, 2010 (left top) Rodney Atkins arrives at Music City Keep On Playin'. *JAE S. LEE*

MAY 16, 2010 (left bottom) Fans wait to see the stars arrive at Music City Keep On Playin'. *JAE S. LEE*

MAY 16, 2010 (opposite) Kimberly Williams and James Denton announce Brad Paisley at Music City Keep On Playin'. *JAE S. LEE*

MAY 16, 2010 (right) Brad Paisley opens the show for Music City Keep On Playin', a benefit for flood relief at the Ryman Auditorium in Nashville. *JAE S. LEE*

MAY 16, 2010 (far right) Brad Paisley opens the show for Music City Keep On Playin', a benefit for flood relief at the Ryman Auditorium in Nashville. *JAE S. LEE*

MAY 16, 2010 (above) Lady Antebellum performs at Music City Keep On Playin', a benefit for flood relief at the Ryman Auditorium in Nashville. *JAE S. LEE*

MAY 16, 2010 (left) Dierks Bentley performs with Sam Bush at Music City Keep On Playin' in Nashville. *JAE S. LEE*

MAY 16, 2010 (right) Martina McBride performs at Music City Keep On Playin' in Nashville. *JAE S. LEE*

MAY 16, 2010 (top) Rodney Atkins performs at Music City Keep On Playin' in Nashville. *JAE S. LEE*

MAY 16, 2010 (above) Kellie Pickler performs at Music City Keep On Playin' in Nashville. *JAE S. LEE*

MAY 16, 2010 (left) Keith Urban performs at Music City Keep On Playin' in Nashville. *JAE S. LEE*

MAY 16, 2010 (opposite) Scrippsnetworks donates $100,000 to Music City Keep On Playin' in Nashville. *JAE S. LEE*

MAY 16, 2010 (above) Academy of Country Music donates a check to Music City Keep On Playin' in Nashville. *JAE S. LEE*

MAY 16, 2010 (opposite left) CeCe Winans performs at Music City Keep On Playin', a benefit for flood relief at the Ryman Auditorium in Nashville. *JAE S. LEE*

MAY 16, 2010 (left) Sheryl Crow performs at Music City Keep On Playin' in Nashville. *JAE S. LEE*

MAY 16, 2010 (left top) Lady Antebellum performs at Music City Keep On Playin', a benefit for flood relief at the Ryman Auditorium in Nashville. *JAE S. LEE*

MAY 16, 2010 (left bottom) Keb' Mo' performs at Music City Keep On Playin', a benefit for flood relief at the Ryman Auditorium in Nashville. *JAE S. LEE*

MAY 16, 2010 (below) Randy Montana performs at Music City Keep On Playin', a benefit for flood relief at the Ryman Auditorium in Nashville. *JAE S. LEE*

MAY 16, 2010 (top left) Dierks Bentley and Brad Paisley perform at Music City Keep On Playin', a benefit for flood relief at the Ryman Auditorium in Nashville. *JAE S. LEE*

MAY 16, 2010 (top middle) Martina McBride blows a kiss to the crowd at Music City Keep On Playin' in Nashville. *JAE S. LEE*

MAY 16, 2010 (right) Jaci Velasquez performs at Music City Keep On Playin', in Nashville. *JAE S. LEE*

MAY 16, 2010 (bottom left) Adam Richman interviews Tony Stewart at Music City Keep On Playin' in Nashville. *JAE S. LEE*

MAY 16, 2010 (left) Will Hoge closes the show at Music City Keep On Playin', a benefit for flood relief at the Ryman Auditorium in Nashville. *JAE S. LEE*

MAY 16, 2010 (far left) Will Hoge closes the show at Music City Keep On Playin' in Nashville. *JAE S. LEE*

THE AFTERMATH

The water has gone down now.

Many of the piles of wet debris have been hauled away, leaving behind wisps of nasty insulation and that haunting smell. Block after block of houses sit empty, stripped to the bones, windows open and fans whirring — their owners are living elsewhere for now.

Two-and-a-half weeks after the worst flood experienced in this lifetime, Nashville is getting back to normal. Tourists are returning. The mayor is wearing a suit again. Ruined gardens are being re-tilled. Some things are evident:

• People are mostly kind. Despite the haters and the grousers and the flame-throwers that clamor for attention, most folks in Middle Tennessee would give you the shirt off their back. Many did just that. It's been amazing to see. If you haven't been moved, your soul is an icicle.

Just one example: A homeowner in one flooded neighborhood has kept the garage door open ever since the flood. Inside are stacks of supplies: bottled water, toothbrushes, bleach, rubber gloves, you name it. A sign on the mailbox says simply, "Take What You Need." People did.

• Mayor Karl Dean will win re-election without blinking, unless something truly unexpected comes into play. Dean, his staff and city employees have done a superior job in calmly leading us through this. The communication was excellent and detailed.

There was no hysteria or useless photo opportunities. From the initial crisis of conserving drinking water to getting building permits, it's gone as smoothly as possible.

• There were unnoticed heroes. The volunteers, of course. But others, too. Such as the owner of A+ Storage who donated warehouse space to the flooded Community Resource Center so it could collect and distribute stuff for flood victims.

• Lessons will be learned. Did Nashville overbuild in the 1980s and 1990s? Did developers push their projects too close to areas that could flood? Why are flooded cars covered by insurance but not flooded houses?

There will be plenty of time for all that down the road.

For now, the water has gone down.

What's left is a big mess, being tackled with faith and hard work, and this cue from our beloved Grand Ole Opry: The show really does goes on, no matter what.

Gail Kerr / The Tennessean

MAY 3, 2010 (left) Keith and Leanne MacDaniel attempt to dry belongings the day after an EF-2 tornado destroyed their home. *MARIANN MARTIN/THE JACKSON SUN*

MAY 4, 2010 (above) Leah Barnett salvages what photographs she can after her house was flooded in the Nations neighborhood in Nashville, TN. *DIPTI VAIDYA*

MAY 3, 2010 (opposite top left) Residents continue tornado damage clean up after an EF-2 tornado hit the Jackson area on Sunday, May 2. *MARIANN MARTIN/THE JACKSON SUN*

MAY 3, 2010 (opposite top right) Reba Surratt's great grandson plays ball amidst the tangled trees in Purdy, TN. Surratt's mobile home was destroyed by an EF-2 tornado. *MARIANN MARTIN/THE JACKSON SUN*

MAY 3, 2010 (opposite bottom left) Debris, including cars, are piled on top of each other after flooding on Antioch Pike near Blue Hole Road. *SHELLEY MAYS*

MAY 3, 2010 (opposite bottom right) Lighthouse Christian School teacher Heather Harrell becomes emotional after finding her grandmother's Bible in her classroom that was destroyed by the flood. The school is located on Antioch Pike. *SHELLEY MAYS*

MAY 4, 2010 (above) Beryl Jack found a few personal items in her mud-soaked trailer in the Antioch Mobile Home Park in Antioch, TN. Trailers were tossed and broken throughout the park. *DIPTI VAIDYA*

MAY 4, 2010 (left top) Beryl Jack enters her home for the first time to retrieve photos in the Antioch Mobile Home Park with landlord Jack Foster in Antioch, TN. *DIPTI VAIDYA*

MAY 4, 2010 (left middle) Allison Patton gets a hug from her sister-in-law, both emotional, as she recovers earrings that her husband, who recently died in February, had given her from her flooded home on Beech Bend Drive in Nashville, TN. *DIPTI VAIDYA*

MAY 4, 2010 (left bottom) A doorway marked with evacuation notes as cleanup and recovery get started on Beech Bend Drive in Nashville, TN. *DIPTI VAIDYA*

MAY 4, 2010 (far left) As the flood waters recede, the clean-up efforts begin in the Richland Creek area near I-40 and Briley Parkway on Delray Dr. as construction worker Manuel Castro cleans the inside of a house. *SAMUEL M. SIMPKINS*

MAY 4, 2010 (top) As the flood waters recede, the clean-up efforts begin in the Richland Creek area near I-40 and Briley Parkway on Delray Dr. as eight year resident Isaac Gallegos picks up the pieces from what he calls a 'pretty much total loss' of his home. Richland Creek rose and then receded Saturday evening, but Sunday's rain flooded early in the morning, when he left. Gallegos added that there might have been a potential looter hanging around Monday afternoon, but nothing was taken. *SAMUEL M. SIMPKINS*

MAY 5, 2010 (above) A house in the Buena Vista neighborhood came completely off its foundation and landed in the middle of the street in Nashville, TN. *DIPTI VAIDYA*

MAY 5, 2010 (left) Damage to Tucker Road in North Nashville is substantial. *LARRY MCCORMACK*

MAY 5, 2010 (above) A home was washed from its foundation and onto Hummingbird Dr. in North Nashville. *LARRY MCCORMACK*

MAY 5, 2010 (above) Tire tracks in the mud left after flood waters receded draw a design on the pavement of a parking lot between First and Second in downtown Nashville. *LARRY MCCORMACK*

MAY 5, 2010 (previous) Furniture, clothes, appliances all line the road as residents try to clean their homes after the flood on West Hamilton Rd. in North Nashville. *LARRY MCCORMACK*

MAY 5, 2010 (above) Janquez Amos, 8, takes a break from cleaning to shoot some hoops as clothes dry in the afternoon sun at his home on West Hamilton Rd. in North Nashville. *LARRY MCCORMACK*

MAY 5, 2010 (left) Water has receded on First Ave. in downtown Nashville. *MANDY LUNN*

MAY 5, 2010 (above) As the water recedes, residents of Pennington Bend return to their homes to get a closer look at the water damage like Charles Lyle who shows the waterline in his home on Steamboat Dr. in the Rivertrace Estates. Many residents said that there was no warning and that the water was about waste deep in about a minute and a half. *SAMUEL M. SIMPKINS*

MAY 5, 2010 (left top) As the water recedes, residents of Pennington Bend return to their homes to get a closer look at the water damage like Adria Campbell, friend of home owners, Tommy Carter and Amy Phillips, as she empties the water out of a box of pictures. *SAMUEL M. SIMPKINS*

MAY 5, 2010 (left bottom) As the water recedes, residents of Pennington Bend return to their homes to get a closer look at the water damage like this big truck. There were a few problems with people going too fast through the area causing a wake and further adding water to belongings in the yards. *SAMUEL M. SIMPKINS*

MAY 5, 2010 (left) James Bryant, a resident of East Nashville, cries in a boat on the way back from his home on Moss Rose after he saw that everything in his home had been destroyed by flood waters. *JOHN PARTIPILO*

MAY 5, 2010 (bottom left) Owners Jack and Jeanne Foster can't believe the total destruction at their Antioch Mobile Home Park in Nashville, TN. Trailers and cars were tossed like matchsticks. *DIPTI VAIDYA*

MAY 5, 2010 (bottom right) Barbara Scivally gives thanks for getting through the flood at the National Day of Prayer in downtown. *JOHN PARTIPILO*

MAY 5, 2010 (above) East Nashville resident Kendric Vance gets ready to be canoed to his home by a volunteer near McGinnis Dr. *JOHN PARTIPILO*

MAY 5, 2010 (left) Residents of an Inglewood neighborhood wait for boats to come pick them up to take them to their flooded homes. *JOHN PARTIPILO*

MAY 5, 2010 (far left) Tammy Awali holds the angel that was at her father's funeral which she salvaged out of her mother's home on McGinnis Street in East Nashville. *JOHN PARTIPILO*

MAY 5, 2010 (left) Janet Stone of Erin, TN, cleans mud off her deceased father's banjo in a creek. Her home now rests under a bridge after flood waters carried the home 400 yards off its foundation. Residents in parts of six middle Tennessee counties were urged to boil water before drinking. *SHELLEY MAYS*

MAY 5, 2010 (above) Furniture, clothes, appliances all go to the road as residents try to clean their homes after recent flooding on West Hamilton Rd. in North Nashville. *LARRY MCCORMACK*

MAY 6, 2010 (above) Downtown from the pedestrian bridge as streets dry out in Nashville, TN. *DIPTI VAIDYA*

MAY 6, 2010 (left top) A mud covered bike in the hard hit Inglewood area in Nashville. *SANFORD MYERS*

MAY 6, 2010 (left bottom) North Nashville. *SAMUEL M. SIMPKINS*

MAY 6, 2010 (opposite) Downtown from the pedestrian bridge as streets dry out in Nashville, TN. *DIPTI VAIDYA*

MAY 6, 2010 (left top) Officer Deacon James Cliff, of the Rose Of Sharon Primitive Baptist Church, shows the damage to the sanctuary to the church, located on Milford Road in North Nashville. The waters were up to the the top of the carport. Everything including the church office, with all the documents, were lost. *SAMUEL M. SIMPKINS*

MAY 6, 2010 (left bottom) Workers clean up flood damage at Mid-South Wire Co. on Visco Dr. *LARRY McCORMACK*

MAY 6, 2010 (opposite) Debrah Loftis gets a hug from her cousin Fred Garrison who helped her gather possessions from her home in Old Hickory. *JOHN PARTIPILO*

MAY 6, 2010 (below) Shawn Courtney, co-owner of Past Perfect, sits in his restaurant and tries to figure out his losses after the basement of their building flooded, destroying their food and inventory in Nashville, TN. 'We're hurting,' said Courtney. Past Perfect is his first restaurant. *DIPTI VAIDYA*

MAY 7, 2010 (right top) Old Hickory Dam. *SAMUEL M. SIMPKINS*

MAY 7, 2010 (right bottom) Old Hickory Dam. Mike Ezell, the Power Shift Operator, talks in the control room at Old Hickory Dam in Hendersonville, TN. *SAMUEL M. SIMPKINS*

MAY 7, 2010 (below) The Harpeth River brought down an electric tower near Shacklett, TN. *DIPTI VAIDYA*

MAY 7, 2010 (above) Cotton's Towing dispatcher Justin Brown shows some of the cars that were submerged by flood waters on I-24. *SHELLEY MAYS*

MAY 7, 2010 (left) The front yard of Cecile James' home on Antioch Pike is covered with waterlogged items from inside her home that was also her business. She isn't sure what to do next but she won't be staying in this home. *LARRY MCCORMACK*

MAY 7, 2010 (top left) Ed Greer, right, surveys the damage in his storage shed with friend E.G. Smith, in Shacklett, TN. Greer's home was destroyed and new boat laid on its side. *DIPTI VAIDYA*

MAY 7, 2010 (top right) Eric Smith Sr. and his son Eric Smith Jr. work to rip up the flooring in his home on Shacklett Ct. in Antioch. Eric Smith Sr. has been living in his car to protect the home from looters. *LARRY McCORMACK*

MAY 7, 2010 (bottom right) Jared McGowan helps rip out a flood destroyed kitchen on Harpeth Bend Rd. in Nashville, TN. *DIPTI VAIDYA*

MAY 7, 2010 (left) Marla Faith looks over some of her paintings that she saved when flood waters ravaged her home and art. *JOHN PARTIPILO*

MAY 7, 2010 (bottom left) Elizabeth Zapp, 84, whose house was destroyed in the flood, cries after seeing the inside of her house. Family and friends and volunteers from as far as Woodbury helped gut her house and others in the area in Shacklett, TN. *DIPTI VAIDYA*

MAY 7, 2010 (bottom right) In an East Nashville neighborhood, Koran Porter, 9, looks over the remains of his guitar, which was destroyed along with many things in his home during the flood. *JOHN PARTIPILO*

MAY 7, 2010 (above) All of these instruments and music gear sit in a warehouse drying out from being under flood waters for 3 days. *JOHN PARTIPILO*

MAY 7, 2010 (opposite left top) A ruined electric guitar. *JOHN PARTIPILO*

MAY 7, 2010 (opposite left middle) Kurt Allison looks at one of his ruined electric guitars while guitar expert Joe Glaser checks the neck on another. *JOHN PARTIPILO*

MAY 7, 2010 (opposite left bottom) Damaged electric guitars dry out

at a warehouse in Nashville. *JOHN PARTIPILO*

MAY 7, 2010 (opposite right) Jerry McPherson checks out one of his guitars that was ruined by flood damage. *JOHN PARTIPILO*

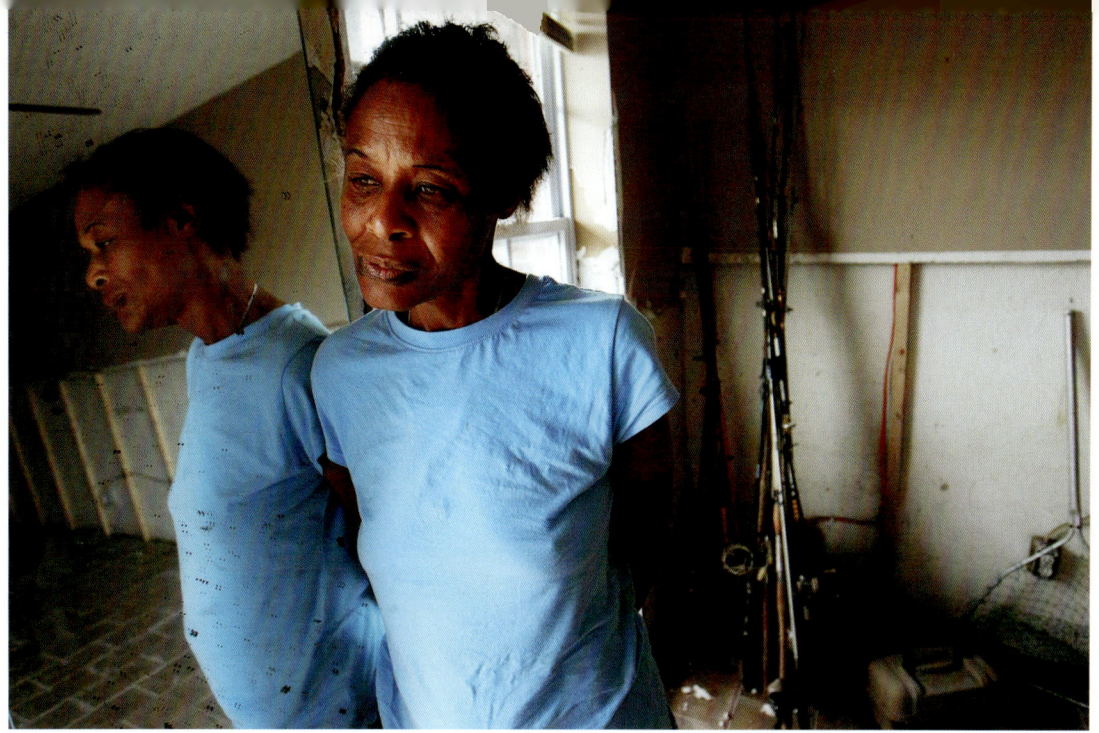

MAY 10, 2010 (left) Theresa Jones, 57, had to leave her apartment because the water was up to her chest. Just a few possessions remain for her. She is hoping that FEMA will visit her soon. *JOHN PARTIPILO*

MAY 10, 2010 (far left) Sherine Sobhi holds neighbor child Jessica Shatat, 10 months, after hanging some laundry out to dry at Millwood Apartments. *JOHN PARTIPILO*

MAY 10, 2010 (below) Judy and Tim Morrison thought they were buying their home in a rent-to-buy agreement until the flood, when they discovered their landlord was not paying for insurance for the property. Now they have lost everything *JOHN PARTIPILO*

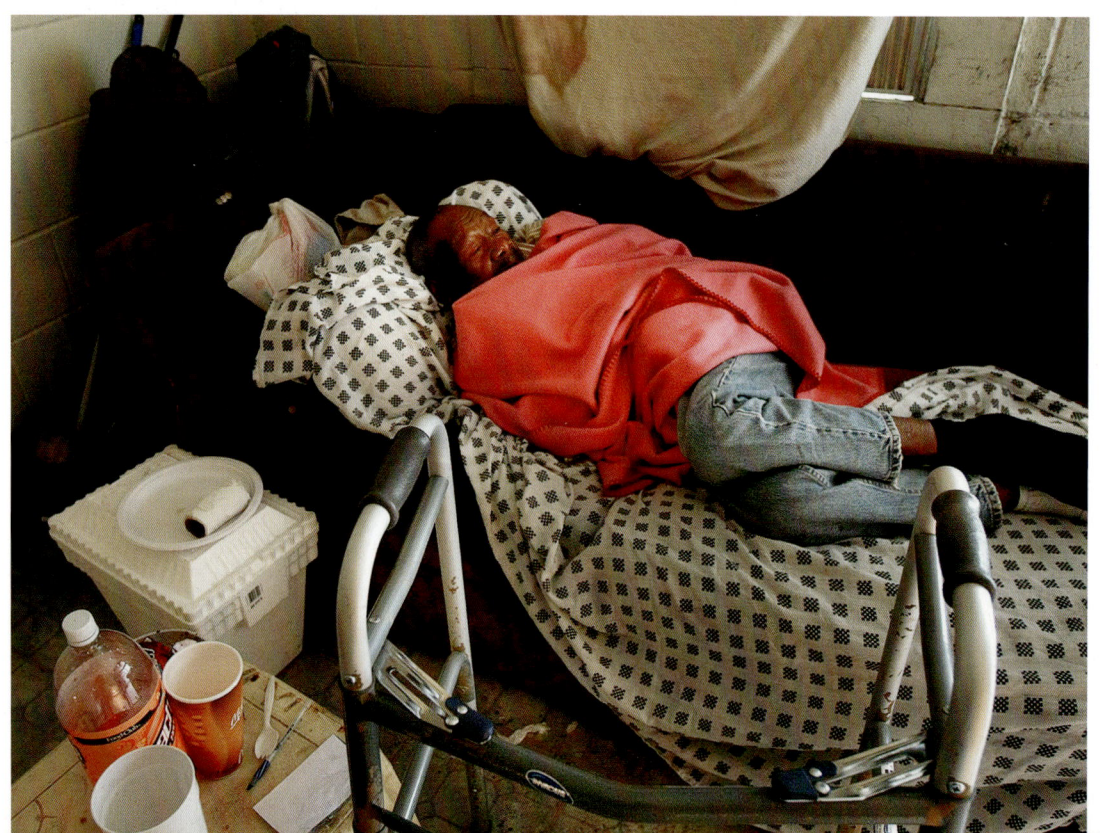

MAY 10, 2010 (above) Charles Schumann of Chicago rests after removing debris from his daughter's Hickman County home, which was destroyed by flood waters. Charleen Wainright's Primm Springs Road home was taken off its foundation by flood waters. The storm washed away bridges, power and water lines in Hickman County. Most of the 20,000 people in the county had no clean water. *SHELLEY MAYS*

MAY 10, 2010 (right top) Kay Mullican talks about how bad it was as the flood waters were rising at her mother's home on Hite St. in West Nashville. As a Fire Dept dispatcher she was sending rescue boats to people all along her mother's street but she didn't know if her mother was still alive. *LARRY MCCORMACK*

MAY 10, 2010 (right bottom) Roy Holt, 88, stayed in his home that was flooded. He had nowhere to go because his wheelchair was destroyed. *JOHN PARTIPILO*

MAY 10, 2010 (far right) A Davidson County Sheriff's work crew picks up debris and other trash as clean-up continues on Hite St. in West Nashville. *LARRY MCCORMACK*

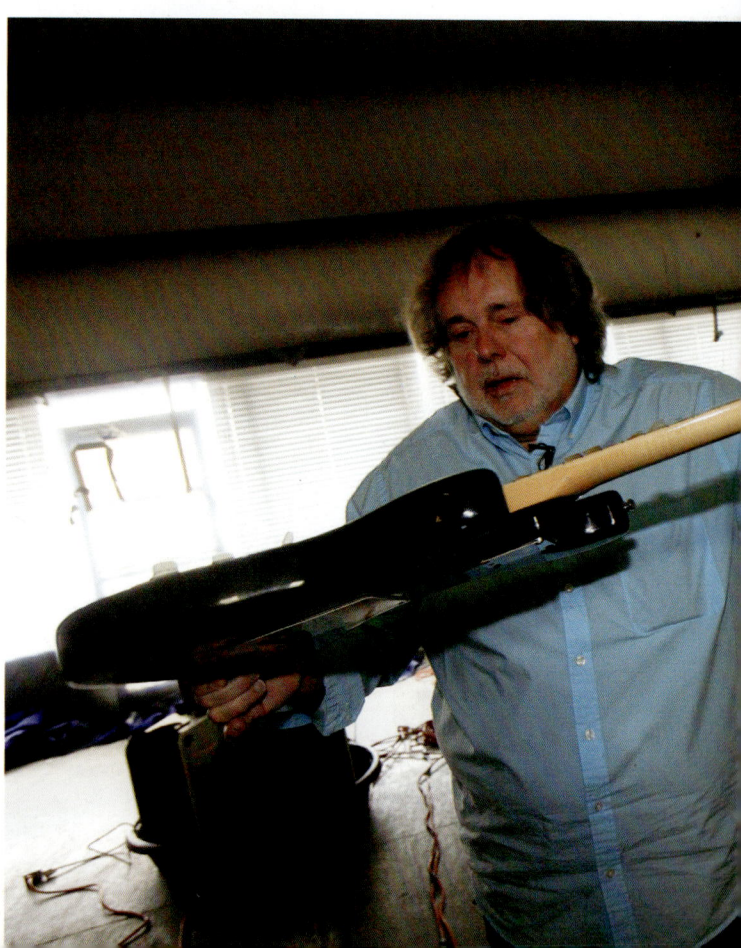

MAY 10, 2010 (opposite top left) KD Wainright,16, and her mother Charleen Wainright take a break from recovering personal items from their Hickman County property. Their home was washed away by flood waters and the family is now living in tents and a loaned RV. Wainright, a Baptist Hospital ER technician, lost three vehicles and her Primm Springs Road home. The storm washed away bridges, power and water lines in Hickman County. *SHELLEY MAYS*

MAY 10, 2010 (opposite top right) Musicians Hall of Fame Founder Joe Chambers shows a Johnny Cash amp that was flooded at Soundcheck and was drying out. Most of these artifacts are irreplaceable. *SAMUEL M. SIMPKINS*

MAY 10, 2010 (opposite bottom left) Charleen Wainright, left, and her son Carson, 13, look at her Nissan Sentra that was carried away by flood waters from her Hickman County home and now rests in a creek full of rocks. *SHELLEY MAYS*

MAY 10, 2010 (opposite bottom right) Musicians Hall of Fame Founder Joe Chambers shows a Charlie McCoy guitar that the water has made chip and peel after being flooded at Soundcheck. *SAMUEL M. SIMPKINS*

MAY 13, 2010 (left top) Rev. Andy Courtney of the Bledsoe Creek Baptist church in Bethpage looks over the water damage in church. The church was hit hard by the flood and was not useable for services. *JOHN PARTIPILO*

MAY 10, 2010 (left bottom) Danny and Janet Stones walk down a creek looking for personal items. The creek flooded and took their home off its foundation, causing it to travel 400 yards down stream. *SHELLEY MAYS*

MAY 12, 2010 (proceeding) A flag is in tatters on the porch amidst flood wreckage on a flood plain on Jamestown Rd. along the Cumberland near Ashland City in Cheatham County, TN. *DIPTI VAIDYA*